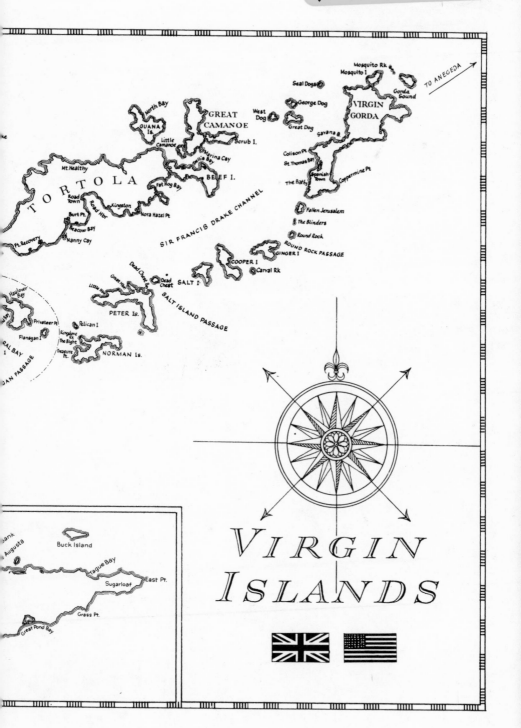

VIRGIN ISLANDS

VIRGIN
ISLANDS

This is a rare sight. *Renegade* ghosting across St. Thomas harbor toward Charlotte Amalie in very light air. It is usually blowing 10 knots or more in here.

VIRGIN ISLANDS

BY

GEORGE T. EGGLESTON

ROBERT E. KRIEGER PUBLISHING COMPANY
HUNTINGTON, NEW YORK
1973

BOOKS BY THE AUTHOR
Orchids on the Calabash Tree
    Virgin Islands
        Tahiti, Voyage Through Paradise

EDITED:
Treasury of Christian Teaching
    Letters from A Saint

Original edition 1959
Revised edition 1973

Printed and published by:

ROBERT E. KRIEGER PUBLISHING CO. INC.
P. O. BOX 542
HUNTINGTON, NEW YORK. 11743

© copyright 1959, 1973
George T. Eggleston

Library of Congress # 59-14615
S. B. N. # 0-88275-087-9

PRINTED IN THE UNITED STATES OF AMERICA

To my daughter
DAY

CONTENTS

CONTENTS

LIST OF ILLUSTRATIONS

LIST OF ILLUSTRATIONS

PUBLISHER'S PREFACE

In the last chapter of this new edition of *VIRGIN ISLANDS* the author has up-dated such of the original material as might be of concern to visiting tourists and yachtsmen sailing to, and through the British and U.S. Virgin Islands. The original story line, recording an unhurried and colorful holiday cruise to every interesting anchorage in the group, has remained unchanged.

When the author revisited the Virgin Islands last he found that they had not only grown in development, population size and accommodations, but offered many more distinctive vacationing joys. Just 3½ hours by jet from New York and 2½ from Miami, The Virgins are exotic islands to visit. While the larger airlines fly to the Islands directly from the U.S. mainland, one may island hop using the amphibians, affectionately called the "Goose," for if you have visited one island you will want to see others. There are many plus factors: While elsewhere in the West Indies, U.S. shoppers are limited to $100 worth of duty-free purchases, including a single bottle of liquor per adult, in the U.S. Virgins, the duty-free exemption is $200, including five fifths (one full gallon) of liquor per adult. Accommodations in the islands range from the luxurious to the very informal. There are big hotels with much in the way of socializing, small ones offering privacy and efficiency motels. The number of rentals in cars and hondas has increased; a driver's license is necessary and it's driving on the *left-hand* side of the road. A passport isn't required and dogs and cats are welcome (provided there has been a rabies vaccination within the last six months). Churches are available of almost all denominations and you can even get married in St. Thomas or St. Croix! The language of the Virgins is English today or "Calypso English" as spoken by the natives, which is a mixture of African and Spanish words, partly from the Scotch influence. The currency is the U.S. dollar.

Columbus discovered the Virgin Islands in 1493 on his second voyage to the New World, and named them in honor of Saint Ursula and her 11,000 virgins. For hundreds of years before Columbus arrived, villages of the peaceful, agricultural Arawak Indians dotted the shores of St. John. At one spot their rock carvings (petroglyphs) mark what must have been a sacred shrine. At the time of discovery, the fierce Caribs, who may have come from South America, barely a century earlier, were encroaching steadily on the Arawak lands. After 1493, Dutch, English, Spanish, French and Danish adventurers came to the Virgin Islands; the Danes first came in the 1670's but did not establish a permanent colony on St. John until 1717. By 1726 all available land on St. John was taken for sugar and cotton plantations. The Danes originally settled the island of St. Thomas by dividing it up into plantations of about 125 acres each, rent to be one turkey per annum delivered to the Governor. Many slaves were imported from Africa by the settlers. These slaves revolted in 1733. The rebellion was finally quelled, but after the outbreak of 1733 the fires of revolt continued to smolder until slavery was abolished in 1848. The act was an economic blow to the planters and contributed to the end of the estates. After a series of unsuccessful negotiations, the United States finally purchased the Danish Islands in 1917 for $25 million.

The U.S. Virgins are three "floating gardens" of tropical America rising from the Caribbean about 1,000 miles southeast of Miami. The appeal of the Islands is based on multiple factors, since each has its own distinctive personality.

Best known of the three "Virgins," to most people, is St. Thomas. Hilly, scenic, and fringed with powdery white beaches, it is rich in things to do and historic places to explore. A good way to capture a "seagull's eye-view" of the island and its lovely port city of Charlotte Amalie is to take the aerial tramway to the top of 1,000-ft. Signal Hill, just above the town. For an equally spectacular view, hire a cab and drive up to Drake's Seat overlooking world-famous Magen's Bay. Sir Francis Drake is said to have used this vantage point to review his fleet. St. Thomas is also headquarters for one of the largest charter fleets in the Caribbean. Should anyone get a hankering to captain his own "cruise ship," everything can be found in Saint Thomas from air-condition U-drive-it houseboats to power cruisers and sailing craft of all types and sizes—with and without crews. Rentals on the larger yachts can run high but are not too steep when several couples band together to share the cost and the fun. There are plenty of fishing stations, too, with experienced skippers ready to take you north of the island to one of the world's finest big-game fishing areas.

Charlotte Amalie, the capital (originally called Tap Hus by the Danes) was once a pirate's lair. The present town perches by the side of a magnificent shell-shaped harbor often accomodating several cruise ships; in fact, it is now the most popular cruise port in the entire West Indies. Visitors do not spoil Saint Thomas because Saint Thomas has been receiving visitors all its life. It has its own character, formed through the years, and maintained in the century-old buildings, the winding streets, the matchless harbor. Those who come to visit and to live have no idea of changing it in their image; they like it as it is. Yet they too are bound to contribute something to the flavor of Saint Thomas, just as did the pirates, the slaves, the Southern rebels of the United States, the trading captains of New England, the Europeans fleeing religious persecution, and all other "visitors" of times gone by who came to St. Thomas on a trip and ended up living there. The shops are lodged in wonderful old warehouses, built to withstand every onslaught of man and nature, and are now one of the Caribbean's most unusual shopping centers. At night, several elegant restaurants serve award-winning cuisine. The narrow byways of Charlotte Amalie throb to a calypso beat, sometimes till dawn.

The Virgin Islanders are very proud of their fast-growing College of the Virgin Islands (CVI). Last year marked the largest enrollment in the history of the college. The St. Thomas campus continues to maintain its "United Nations character" with students representing countries from all over the world. Additionally, full-time students come from over 17 states and the District of Columbia on the U. S. mainland. The most popular baccalaureate program at the college continues to be teacher education. In addition there is continued enrollment in business administration, social sciences, mathematics, nursing, humanities, pre-medical technology, pre-pharmacy and pre-engineering, accounting, executive secretarial administration, hotel and restaurant management, construction technology and police science and administration. A Center for Marine and Environmental Sciences is under construction. The college which started in 1963 is proud too of their campus on St. Croix.

A short flight southward from St. Thomas lies St. Croix, 84 square miles in area and the largest of the U. S. Virgins. Somewhat more sedate than its northern neighbor, St. Croix still boasts plenty of tropic night spots and gaiety, particularly during the lively Christmas-New Year Festival period when "everyone" is on holiday! There are also many fine hotels, guest houses and restaurants and the free-port shopping exists as on St. Thomas: but the shops in Christiansted and Frederiksted are often less crowded. The "big" island is also full of surprises. Its northwest side is lushly tropical, with its own jungle rain forest. But 23 miles away, at the eastern end, the landscape becomes almost as arid as a desert and is filled with cactus, succulents and exotically beautiful flowers. Between lies rolling green countryside, once the site of the great Danish sugar plantations, most of which have fallen into picturesque decay. One plantation home, however, is well worth a visit. It is Whim Greathouse. The Greathouse, located about two miles east of Frederiksted, has been restored to an approximation of its original elegance and is indeed a showplace; a house museum which recreates the opulent life of the sugar planters with fine furniture, silver and china brought out from Europe in the late 1700's when the island was at the peak of its prosperity. Among Saint Croix's many other attractions are two outstanding ones: No golfer worth his salt would miss Fountain Valley, ranked as one of the five greatest championship golf courses in the world, and one of the most beautiful. And then there's the now famous Buck Island Reef National Monument, an uninhabited storybook island within an hour's sail of Christiansted. It is a thrilling experience; the swimming is superb but more exciting still is the snorkeling over Buck Island's marked underwater trail, watching the friendly, incredibly colored fish dart in and out among the undersea coral gardens. If you are without a boat, the charter boats and glass bottom boats provide the necessary snorkeling equipment, and, if you swim, within a few minutes you will feel like a pro. The sailing is beautiful here and the Trimaran has become an increasingly popular class in these waters because of their shallow draft. In Christiansted, the town square and waterfront have been restored to bring back a sunny day of the 18th Century. The ancient streets reflect the settlement of the Danish, French, Dutch, English and Spaniards. The old fort, with its canons aimed at the sea, has a history to relate all of its own. On the western side of the island is the old and charming town of Frederiksted, with quaint shops and a true-feeling of non-commercialism. There is a group of U. S. mainland people there who work the restaurants and motels and who have found a new, and to them, beautiful life.

Last, but certainly not least, of the three U. S. Virgin Islands is the smallest, and regarded as the most beautiful, **and** least developed one, St. John (the "Escapists' Island"). Although only minutes by seaplane or ferry from bustling St. Thomas, it has the remote Garden-of-Eden feeling of a Pacific Bali H'ai. St. John is for the true nature lover, the person who dotes on jungle-clad hills and curving, deserted beaches, Indian artifacts (many are still being discovered). All of this is more easily understood when we realize that two-thirds of St. John has been set apart as a U. S. National Park. Swimming, fishing, snorkeling and underwater photography are fast-growing sports. Equipment can be rented, serviced, or purchased on St. Thomas, Sailboats and other small craft can also be rented. Roads on the island are unimproved, but jeep taxi service is available, and scheduled jeep and boat tours begin in St. Thomas, Royal Road (Centerline), extending from Cruz Bay on the west to Coral Bay on the east. Among the highlights are Coral Bay Overlook, Trunk Bay Beach, Annaberg Ruins and Reef Bay Valley. Accommodations on St. John are extremely limited. The largest guest facility is Caneel Bay Plantation, a non-profit conservation established by the Rockefeller family. There are double rooms, cottages, and groceries, hardware, restaurants and laundry facilities are available.

North and east of St. John lie the British Virgin Islands and the Sir Francis Drake Channel—the scenic highway for yachtsmen. The passage is bordered by rugged islands, largest of which is Tortola, now becoming tourist oriented. Road Town is the capital and principle port. All visitors touching land in the British Virgin Islands must first clear British customs and immigration, usually a fast, painless procedure. Visitors need no passport and American money is the accepted currency. South of Tortola and east of St. John are many smaller islands, virtually uninhabited. This is the paradise for yachtsmen—deep water, protected coves and good trade winds. On Norman Island are the caves rising from the sea, where an islander some 50 years ago found a chest of gold. Continuing east, is Peter Island and Dead Chest Bay. Legend says a pirate captain marooned 15 buccaneers there, giving rise to the ditty, "Fifteen Men on the Dead Man's Chest." Beyond Peter Island is Salt Island, a heaven for scuba divers. On the south side is the site of the wreck of the *Rhone*. Here, more than a hundred years ago, the large vessel *Rhone* sank in

30 to 90 feet of water. And then there are Baths on the southern tip of the Virgin Gorda. The Baths are impressive—giant boulders of granite jumbled in arches over crystal-clear pools. A dip in the limpid water within the chambers, amidst the unusual pilings of rock, is unforgettable. The largest island north of Virgin Gorda is Anegada, a long, flat expanse ringed by dangerous reefs and coral heads. It is a promised land for scuba divers, rod and reel fishermen, and spearfishermen, but yachtmen avoid it as a graveyard of ships.

Half of the beauty of the Virgin Islands is underwater. There are excellent diving conditions for all, from the beginner to the experienced diver; instructors and guides are available, as well as all necessary equipment for rental. The best sailing in the world awaits you in the Virgin Islands. You'll find crystal-clear waters, protected anchorages, steady breezes, year-round sun, perfect climate, good boats and breathtaking scenery. Nothing has changed about this. The trade winds are strongest in the winter and spring, with lighter breezes in summer and early fall (mean temperature 78 degrees). Big-game fishermen from everywhere in the world swoop down on the three U. S. Virgins to establish new world records. And the Virgins always reward someone; if not with a new world record, then with an authentic story of the one that got away! Reliable sightings indicate that the Atlantic Blue marlin in the 1,000 pound category are hungry. You'll find dolphin, wahoo, kingfish, tuna, barracuda, bonito, sailfish and more. There are charter captains and natives to show you the proper setting of reel and tackle. There are two angling clubs, the Virgin Island Game Fishing Club in Saint Thomas and the St. Croix Sport Fishing Club. Sloops, yawls, ketches, schooners, cutters are all available.

CHAPTER I

ST. THOMAS

THE plane banked gracefully, seat belt and no-smoking lights flashed on for a landing, and the pretty West Indian stewardess gave the little speech warning intransit passengers that the stop-over would be twenty minutes and transit passengers that they must not leave anything behind.

We had been flying through a rain-squall and the southwestern shore of St. Thomas below us was slightly grayed with mist. This was unusual for an island where the hotel slogans say "If the sun does not shine today you do not pay." It looked rather like the beginning of one of those rainy weekends on Long Island Sound when cruising yachts sit out two or three days at Block Island waiting for the fog bank to roll back. Hazel suggested it might be fun to have a free suite at the Virgin Isle Hilton, one of the most expensive hostelries in the world.

I pressed my face against the plane's window and looked down hoping the sun would make a sudden break-through and reveal the familiar sapphire shallows and purple coral heads off the airport. All was gray and lifeless, but visibility was fair enough, as it always is in these blessed islands, where aside from hurricanes there are none of the weather horrors of northern climes.

I had about ten seconds to spot it. Near a tiny cay* just off Lindbergh Bay a yacht with all sails flying was on a rock-studded shoal. Her

* Pronounced: Key.

[1]

In this view from the heights overlooking Charlotte Amalie and St. Thomas harbor, two cruise ships are at dockside and one is anchored off. The marina at Yacht Haven is at extreme left.

bow was high and her cockpit was buried in a lather of breaking sea. I expected everybody in the plane to be talking about it as we disembarked. But everybody including Hazel had missed it.

I tried to make conversation about what I had seen as we were languidly passed through customs.

"There's a sailboat on the rocks out there," I said as I showed our passports to the customs official.

"Oh, we have little boats on the rocks all the time around here," he laughed.

"But this looks like a 60 or 70 foot yacht."

"Well, that's what we call a little boat," he laughed again.

A half hour later our taxi had deposited us at Yacht Haven and we had the driver wait while we went to the dock-side to ascertain the whereabouts of *Renegade*. On the bulletin board was a message addressed to us saying that *Renegade* would be in to take us aboard two days hence. Eunice Boardman, her owner, was presently doing some underwater photography near Virgin Gorda some thirty miles east of St. Thomas.

I asked a lounging skipper in a battered white yachting cap if he had heard anything about the grounded boat off the airport.

"That's the old *Lystria*," he said. "She belongs to Christine Cromwell Christiansen. The Coast Guard took everybody off."

My informant excused himself and walked off to answer a ringing telephone. The mystery seemed to be deepening. As Hazel and I taxied back into town for a couple of days of sightseeing the heavens cleared and Caribbean sunshine took over to return everything to the accustomed dazzling brightness.

We had last done some sailing in the Virgin Islands on a springtime cruise. March, April and May in the Caribbean is the dry season when all the greenery has turned to brown. Our present cruise was commencing in October. The rainy season, the hurricane months preceding our arrival, had been the wettest in many years. The islands dotting the horizon as far as the eye could see were lush and green. It is too bad that most visitors come to the Virgins only in the winter months. True, they get away from the worst months up north. But they never see the Virgins at their best, during the post-hurricane season when things are green and island life is at its quietest non-tourist pace.

When you come to St. Thomas bring your driver's license. By showing it and presenting a dollar bill to a clerk in the old fort near the center of Charlotte Amalie* you have a visitor's permit entitling you to drive the network of scenic roads which wander all over the island. A car may be rented at $8.80 per day and you need not worry too much about the problem of driving on the left. The locals expect some confusion and watch out for you.

We first drove up, up, and up, behind the town and harbor and sought out Drake's seat, the spot where local legend tells us the Elizabethan sea-dog used to sit telescope in hand and contemplate the archipelago stretching east and northward. Before we passed over the top of the island we parked and looked back over the harbor and toward the southern horizon where the big sister island of St. Croix lay in sharp profile forty miles away. The roof tops of Charlotte Amalie sparkled below us in the mid-morning sunlight. Off to the left, adjoining the great docks of the West India Company, the impressive fleet of yachts swung to their moorings at Yacht Haven. Directly below us at the market docks a row of out-island sloops and schooners were unloading vegetables, fruits and fish. Several native sloops dotted the harbor reaching in and reaching out across the brisk northeast trades. The two large islets that protect the anchorage from the south and west, Hassel and Water Isles, looked strangely uninhabited for a region in the throes of one of the biggest real estate booms in history.

As we started our slow descent down the windward side looking for the historic landmark we suddenly heard shouting above us.

"Drake seat, Drake seat, Drake seat."

And then a burst of calypso in a highly pitched twang accompanied by something that sounded slightly like a bass fiddle.

As we parked the car on the edge of a precipice that looked out over an incredibly blue and beautiful bay three youngsters waved to us from a stone seat above the road. They were colored lads of about eight, ten and twelve years. The eldest, the leader, wore a baseball cap and played an orange-colored plastic ukulele. The middle one had as strange a con-

* Pronounced: Am-al-ye.

The three troubadours we met at Drake's Seat high above Magen's Bay had a fine repertoire of calypso songs. The lad at center twanged his wash tub bass viol with amazing skill.

As one faces westward across St. Thomas Harbor, Hassel Isle's water catchment is prominent at left. The massive Virgin Isle Hilton is directly above line-up of Tortola sloops at the quayside.

traption as we had ever seen. From the center of the bottom of an over-turned wash tub was a well resined cord which was held taut by a stick which rested on the tub. When the boy twanged up and down the cord the instrument produced the bass viol sounds we heard. The littlest boy beat the tub with a twig. We thought the music was better than a lot we had heard in Trinidad. But it didn't produce just the atmosphere we had in mind for a meditation at Drake's seat. We payed them well and suggested they go away for half an hour.

Drake surely must have had a great sense of beauty as well as sense for naval tactics. Legend has it that he sat here to study the sailing pattern of incoming caravels from Spain as they tacked downwind through the island-flanked passage that is now known as Sir Francis Drake Channel. But the doughty navigator must have at times let his mind wander to the lovely coves, bights and inlets at every hand and especially the immediate anchorage before him, now called Magens Bay. One wonders if he might not have said to himself, as countless Americans have said upon beholding this unspoiled spot, "Oh to build a house over there above that beach and settle down for the rest of my life." He may have looked at the close-by little sister island of St. John and decided, as Laurance Rockefeller did almost four hundred years later, that such a beautiful island should never be spoiled. It should by royal decree be made a Crown preserve and set aside as a public park for all to enjoy.

Where are the Virgin Islands? Until recently many an American thought they were somewhere in the Bahamas or part of Puerto Rico. Or that they had something to do with divorces or rum, or both. Sir Algernon Aspinwall in his venerable POCKET GUIDE TO THE WEST INDIES says that once during a debate in Commons about an appropriation for the British Virgins one honorable member admitted that the only statement he could make regarding their locale was that they must be as far as conceivable from the Isle of Man.

Columbus was the first European to know anything about the Virgins. He discovered them on his second voyage in 1493 and called them "Las Virgenes" in honor of the eleven thousand virgins of St. Ursula who died resisting a hord of barbarian rapists. The islands, vaguely suggesting thousands of recumbant nudes, are not as numerous as Columbus' naming would suggest. The American Virgins consist of the three principal islands of St. Thomas, St. John and St. Croix with about fifty adjacent islets and rocks. They lie about forty miles east and south of Puerto Rico and fourteen hundred miles from New York.

The islands were long owned by Denmark, but as far back as the Civil War the U. S. was aware of their value as a possible U. S. Naval depot, commanding as they do the most important sea approaches from the Atlantic to the Caribbean. Lincoln and William Seward actually started negotiations for their purchase in 1863. Denmark was then in need of cash because of her defeat in war with Prussia and Austria and was willing to sell the Virgins cheap. A plebiscite was held in the islands which showed the inhabitants to be overwhelmingly in favor of the change. Everything was in order. That is almost everything. The U. S. Senate abruptly refused to ratify the proposal and negotiations were subsequently broken off.

It wasn't until 1914 that the matter was seriously considered again by the U. S. With the outbreak of World War I Secretary of State Lansing pointed out to President Wilson that if Germany won the war she was sure to insist on a foothold in the Caribbean. To secure St. Thomas Harbor, a base capable of holding the entire World War I U. S. fleet, a treaty was concluded with the Danes for all their Caribbean holdings. Again a favorable plebiscite was held. This was duly ratified by the Senate and the Danish Rigsdag, and formal transfer took place March 31, 1917. The tab which Uncle Sam picked up was for $25,000,000, five times the figure the sagacious Lincoln had arranged.

The British Virgin Islands have been continuously under the Union Jack since 1672. They commence almost a stone's throw beyond St. John and extend to form the eastern extremity of the Greater Antilles. Besides numbers of small rocks and half submerged reefs there are thirty-six islands of which only eleven are inhabited. Road Town on the largest island Tortola, is the official port of entry and only town in the British group. This is the capital and residence of the Administrator of the British Virgins and has a population of about twelve hundred. We had anchored briefly at Road Town during an earlier cruise. But we had then sailed by the others, Anegada,

Virgin Gorda, Fallen Jerusalem, Beef, Salt, Peter, Norman and Dead Man's Chest, resolving to come back for a really thorough look.

Now as we sat at Drake's seat eyeing the U. S. and British Virgins as they stretched eastward, we laid out a little plan for our cruise. We would proceed out of Yacht Haven to circle St. Thomas clockwise, poking in and out of the places that interested us most, anchoring in the spots we thought should be described in most detail for the visiting yachtsman. We would then circumnavigate St. John following the same procedure. Then Norman, Peter, Tortola, Salt, Beef, Guana, The Camanoes and Virgin Gorda. Coming back we would case some of the anchorages we had missed outbound and once back at St. Thomas we would cross south to St. Croix and conclude our voyage.

We took another whole day driving our little rental Volkswagen up hill and down dale crossing and recrossing the island orienting ourselves to everything ashore. We made several trips to Yacht Haven and talked over the radio telephone of one of the charter yachts to *Renegade* as she came closer to the rendezvous with us.

At precisely 8:28 on the morning of Friday, October 3rd, as we sat on our balcony at Hotel 1829 enjoying our breakfast, the white sails and coral-red hull of *Renegade,* came sliding around Muhlenfels Point. By the time *Renegade* had tacked twice to make her anchorage in Yacht Haven at the head of Long Bay we had checked out of our hotel and were on our way to join her.

Our reunion was a joyous one. We had last seen Eunice when we sailed across the St. Lucia channel with her for a short holiday in Martinique some five months before. Over escargots and tenderloins at Etienne's we had talked not only of someday sailing the Virgins together but of other concentrated archipelagos of island paradises for other somedays.

A few words here about Eunice and *Renegade.* She and her husband, Andrew, had had *Renegade* custom-built in Germany. A steel-hulled ketch, fifty feet overall, *Renegade* is one of John Alden's finest conceptions of what a small ocean cruising yacht should be.

[9]

After Eunice and her husband took possession of the boat at the Abeking and Rasmussen yard in Germany they made a seven thousand mile cruise that took them to the North Cape, six hundred miles above the Arctic Circle. Never before had an American yacht ventured so far north. Later, on this cruise, they spent weeks sailing among the Norwegian fjords. All this they did without benefit of crew.

In Bremen, Eunice and her husband agreed to separate and Eunice took a skeleton crew from the shipyard and skippered *Renegade* across the Atlantic to the West Indies. She soon made a reputation for knowing as much about the harbors, reefs, shoals, rocks and out-of-the-way anchorages in both the U.S. and British Virgins as any skipper in the area. *Renegade's* ship-shape condition reflected her constant attention to every detail, topside and below.

After exchanging greetings with Eunice, we shook hands with Felix and Rufus, *Renegade's* able bodied seamen. They are both St. Lucia boys in their early twenties and either one can lift a hundred pound kedge anchor as though it were made of balsa wood. Felix is an all-round sailor and can reef, hand or steer with the best. Rufus' specialty is cooking and he can turn out delectable meals on schedule in any kind of going. Both can go hand over hand up a coconut tree or up the rigging with the wires between their toes as though jet propelled.

The final member of the ship's company was *Skipperkey,* a small black Belgian Barge dog. The breed is called Schipperke which means little skipper in Belgian. Schipperkes are only happy when afloat and prefer the company of people to their own kind.

With so many mouths to feed the business of stocking *Renegade* for a month's cruising is quite a challenge. Once clear of St. Thomas' supermarket and the little shops of St. John and Tortola's Road Town we would be strictly on our own. We spent most of the first morning buying and stowing supplies. St. Thomas' prices on canned goods and other stateside foods are about 20% above U. S. figures. Lettuce was 52¢ per head, tomatoes were 15¢ each. Ten dozen eggs, seventy-five cans of soup. Steaks, chops, hamburger, bacon, ham, cheese, bread, crackers—the list seemed endless. The matter of feeding Felix and Rufus was the biggest problem. They worked hard and ate as though their stomachs were bottomless pits. They didn't care so much what they ate just so they had

Renegade came alongside the West India Company docks for water. This is the eastern end of St. Thomas harbor showing the yacht anchorage in the middle distance and Bluebeard's Castle Hotel above, center.

quantity. They would follow four pounds of hamburger with two loaves of bread. They relished a platter full of rice as much as a dozen scrambled eggs. Underway they would be cooking for themselves all the time, so to anticipate this drain on the larder we put twenty-five pounds of rice and fifty pounds of beans aboard. We also presented each with a spear gun to encourage them into the sea for fish.

Many West Indians are natural born under-water fishermen and in most cases have followed this hobby using only the crudest of home-made equipment. Given the first class gear that Eunice carried aboard *Renegade* Felix and Rufus could be expected to establish some sort of a record. They managed to supply us with fresh fish at almost every anchorage.

For many years the best drinking water to be had at St. Thomas was at the docks of the West India Company next to Yacht Haven. Here the cruising yachtsman would be greeted by a small, leathery-faced colored man who wore a baseball cap over a shock of unmanageable hair and called out in a high-pitched voice, "Here is de hose—My name's Hodge, and I'm de head water boy around here." Hodge was quite a character and liked to boast when the company tanks were full "We got twenty thousan' gallons of water under this here dock." After a heavy rainy season when his tanks were full he used to offer to hose off a yacht's decks as a bonus. The water those days was $2.00 a ton, with a minimum charge of $2.00 even if a yacht's tanks only held 50 gallons.

All this was in the old days when U.S. Navy barges used to bring water from San Juan to St. Thomas during the seasonal months of drought.

Today all this has changed. Visiting yachts calling at Yacht Haven for fuel or dockage can draw freely on an unlimited supply of water piped through the lines of the public water system. The Virgin Islands Corporation at first planned for a sea-water distillation plant which would deliver some 200,000 gallons of drinking water daily. This, together with the help of the old rain-water catchments was thought to be an ample supply. The original plan was to operate a 2,500 Kilowatt generator in conjunction with the desalinization plant.

Today at a cost of much more than the original estimate of $3,000,000 a highly efficient water-producing complex is capable of delivering some 2,000,000 gallons per day. A yacht calling at a Marina for water only, is charged at the rate of about 35 cents for 100 gallons. This is quite a change from former times when old residents complained that the mere flushing of a toilet cost as much as two packs of cigarettes.

Skipperkey, with ten generations of barge dog pedigree behind her, has an inborn resentment for the fuss and flurry of putting on sail. She is in her element when *Renegade* is running along monotonously with the big diesel going. *Skipperkey* tore around the deck barking and making passes at everyone's ankles as mizzen, mainsail, staysail and jib went up. Once sails were set she found a shaded nook at the base of the mainmast and curled up and went disgustedly to sleep. This was a final gesture of disdain, for barge dogs make a practice of patrolling cockily from bow to stern, never resting when a non-heeling vessel is under foot. *Skipperkey's* attitude was quite out of tune with the high morale of the rest of the ship's company. *Renegade* had a brand new suit of Dacron sails that fitted as smoothly as a cup defender's. Of interest to yachtsmen is a note about the purchase of these sails. A dozen leading sailmakers in America and England had been asked for bids. Abeking and Rasmussen delivered the sails in St. Thomas for $1000, just $500 less than the next lowest bidder.

Even for those who have sailed a lot in Caribbean waters the reliability of the old familiar northeast tradewind is a constant source for wonder. It may shift more to east or a bit to south. It may pipe up to twenty-five or thirty knots. It may pipe down to twelve or fifteen. But only on rare occasions does it cease to blow enough to carry masted vessels to their destinations with a relentless regularity matched only by death and taxes.

We sailed across St. Thomas harbor to the tip of Hassel Island as half a dozen Tortola sloops were reaching for the market docks below the city on our right. These native boats are rather crude when close up but at a couple of hundred yards look very graceful if not downright yachty. They have a sense of fun, too, and although these were in the business of carrying produce they were actually racing each other and the little fleet looked like part of a regatta. Two waved us off when we threatened to steal their wind.

When we passed around the northern tip of Hassel Isle within the harbor we were off Cha Cha Town, the home of a remarkably energetic race of people. These are descendants of immigrants from the French is-

Viewed from the heights above Charlotte Amalie the entrance to St. Thomas Harbor is clearly seen at left. The long piece of land stretching across the picture behind Signal Hill is Water Isle

land of St. Barts who came to St. Thomas in the 1850's and brought their skills of basket making, hat making and fishing with them. They have not intermingled with other groups and still speak a language deriving from Norman French. Just after leaving Cha Cha Town to starboard we passed through the very narrow entrance into West Gregorie Channel picking up the Water Isle buoy to port and passing the submarine docks lining Little Krum Bay on our starboard hand. When charging along with a bagful of wind one gets the impression that there might be hidden dangers everywhere. To offset any such emotion of trepidation it is appropriate to quote here from the U. S. Coast Pilot. "St. Thomas is almost surrounded by small islands and cays, in general bold and steep-to, with but very few hidden dangers to guard against."

We were amazed at the size of Water Isle. It looked more like a king size island than the tiny tropical resort islet we had pictured in our minds after reading the travel folders. The island is almost two miles long and rather bare looking with large patches of low underbrush covering parts of it. The terrain is rolling and the highest points are around three hundred feet. We anchored in Druif Bay finding twelve feet of water about one hundred yards from a white sand beach at the center of the bay. A cement cabana here is easy to line up with.

Druif Bay

Druif Bay is well protected except from the west and has a good holding bottom of sand. Hazel and I dinghied ashore and the only person around, a woman wrapped from head to foot in a large beach towel, directed us to a path leading up to the hotel. The woman had been bathing and was curled up in a beach chair at the cabana. She said, "I'm not trying to hide from anyone in this towel. It's simply that the sand flies are biting."

Some people attract beach bugs wherever they go in the Caribbean. Hazel and I have never been bothered by these stinging insects.

It was a hot uphill climb to the hotel but we were rewarded by the view of *Renegade* sitting like a queen in the center of the little blue bay.

On the Water Isle hotel dining verandah we found the owners, Walter and Floride Phillips, having tea with a couple of young honeymooning guests. The Phillipses were an attractive friendly pair and found they had a booming business on their hands following a glowing magazine story about them and their enterprise, complete with a spread of color pictures. They originally got involved in Water Isle in 1951 when they first saw it and fell in love with it. In 1953 they signed a forty year lease with the U.S. Department of the Interior and started converting the abandoned army buildings into the components of a hotel. Both Phillipses had held lucrative jobs in New York, he in Wall Street, she as a buyer for Lord and Taylor. They had saved their money, and decided as they reached their fifties to exchange the high-tension living and awful climate of the north for a new life in the tropics. They had not since regretted their decision. But if they had it to do over again they might not have selected such a large piece of real estate for their idyllic isle.

The Phillipses had spent large sums of money adapting the abandoned government installations on the island to their own purposes. They inherited some $3,000,000 worth of old underground forts, above-ground administration buildings, seven miles of road, and a rain catchment system connected to a 250,000 gallon reservoir. All this looked like an asset on the books but presented tremendous headaches in the way of maintenance and repairs.

The Operation was, however, not all outgo. Mr. Warren Corning, a stateside tycoon who had bought some three hundred thirty-eight acres at Botany Bay, St. Thomas, for $500,000, also took over the leasehold of one hundred acres of Water Isle for $100,000. The Phillipses had sold several plots to friends and acquaintances for $3,000 an acre and upward and thanks to the magazine article they were deluged with inquiries by mail.

The Phillipses still had over two hundred acres to play with. One of the hidden assets which they had no use for was an underground fort with several big rooms connected to a gun emplacement that commands a bluff overlooking the sea. One of their enterprising friends had talked of leasing this and going into the wholesale mushroom business.

At Providence Point, before we entered Druif Bay, we saw the cruiser the Phillipses used to ferry their guests and supplies from the Water Isle dock at Submarine Base. It took five minutes to cross the channel and the boat

This 448 pound blue marlin was taken off St. Thomas by Mr. Frank Miller, a visiting tourist, in September 1971. Mr. Miller did it using a 12 pound test line thereby setting up a new world record.

Bluebeard's Castle hotel on St. Thomas is a much photographed landmark. There are many conflicting legends as to its history.

carried hotel guests free on an hourly schedule. About the only complaint the Phillipses had with their island was that it is hard to pronounce the word Druif. Nobody knows what the word means and most people think it is a misspelling of Druid. They have unofficially changed Druif Bay to Honeymoon Bay and Druif Point to Rainbow Point.

There were a couple of jeeps on Water Isle and we were given a ride to Flamingo Point on the southern tip where a high bluff looks over a breaking surf. From here one gets a spectacular view of the islands to the east. But to us the most startling sight was to the west. There on Flat Cays, a couple of miles across West Gregorie channel, lay *Lystria* with some shreds of her headsails still fluttering in the breeze. The story, as the Phillipses had it, was that two mechanics were the only persons aboard when one of her plates caved in and she started to sink. They left her in a dinghy without bothering to take the sails down and she sailed herself onto the rocks at Flat Cays. The mystery continued to deepen.

By the time we were off Flat Cays the wind had picked up so that a heavy chop was slamming against the rocks. We sailed off and on for a half hour taking pictures of one of the saddest sights one can ever behold, a yacht being pounded to pieces and nobody trying to do anything about it.

From Flat Cays to the western tip of St. Thomas we were on a broad reach. Here we sailed in close leaving West Cay and Salt Cay to starboard, rounding Salt Cay to turn eastward into Salt Cay passage. Dutchcap Cay, Cockroach Island and Cricket Rock were easily defined to port.

Now we were close hauled and the sailing really began. There simply is no better sailing in the world than doing just what we were doing. To try to elaborate would be meaningless. As we stood into the open sea a flock of brown boobies picked us up and the antics of these birds can be studied with fascination by the hour. They circled us, glided behind us and at times dove all around us. There were always two or three flying in so close we could almost reach out and touch them. For ten minutes I stood in the bow leaning out over the pulpit and studied one's olive-blue bill and non-blinking eye as he effortlessly flew and glided just a few feet away. *Renegade* is an exceptionally dry boat. Although we were slamming into quite a rolling sea very little spray came aboard.

Boobies are technically called gannets. They were nicknamed boobies because sailors considered them stupid for allowing themselves to be easily caught. When they make a landing, which they sometimes do on a ship's deck, they make no effort to fly off when approached and captured. Perhaps they are just lazy, or like the wild birds in far away places do not fear man.

I thought perhaps they were following us the way gulls do, looking for a handout of bread or left-over scraps. But they eat only the fish of the sea and according to the bird books they follow a vessel hoping to dive for fish which will be disturbed by its passage. Every so often as *Renegade's* hull obligingly turned up some food we were treated to some spectacular diving. Boobies commonly dive for fish from heights of sixty to one hundred feet above the surface of the sea and often pursue their quarry under water to depths of almost one hundred feet.

MAGENS BAY

Just before sunset we entered Magens Bay. Outer Brass and Inner Brass Islands on our starboard looked like one island as we first picked them up. As we entered Magens we favored the western side to avoid Ornen Rock which has only six feet of water over it. *Renegade* draws seven. It is hard to keep remembering that the depths on the charts of these waters mean what they say. Tides here amount to hardly a foot.

Once inside we favored the eastern side of the bay and anchored in twelve feet about thirty yards from the northern end of the beach. It was still light enough to see each link of our chain and the anchor on the sandy bottom. We had a swim, cocktails and some very fine hamburger steaks which Rufus produced with hashed brown potatoes and a mixed vegetable salad on the side. All this was topped off with fresh fruit and coconut salad that had been in a big jar on the ice all day. We were all in our bunks by eight o'clock and slept very well indeed in spite of the constant roll which is considered by some to be the main drawback for anchoring in Magens overnight.

Next morning we were all up at dawn and in full agreement with the St. Thomas travel folders that Magens Bay is one of the most beautiful spots in the world. It had awed us from Drake's seat but in a different way. From our anchorage we seemed to be on a large lake, because due to the perspective the entrance behind us narrowed until it was almost closed in by Outer Brass Island sitting almost five miles away. There is supposed to be a shoal across the bay two-thirds of the way in and covered by only five feet of water. Hazel and I took the dinghy and made soundings from where we lay right in to where the boulders of the north shore join the beach and found plenty of water right up to a biscuit's toss off. The chart shows a big pot hole of over six fathoms here.

The white sand beach at the head of the bay is open to the public and for a small fee there is a little dressing room available for changing. The beach is almost a mile long and they say that sometimes it is quite busy in the tourist season. But the several times we have been there it was deserted. Oddly enough Magens is one of the few bays in the Virgins where Eunice had never before anchored. The windward shores of these islands are not particularly favored by yachts because of the aforementioned roll.

Eunice was curious about the fish life, if any, in the Bay and we took masks, snorkels and inflated mattresses and went along the rocky north shore about a mile studying the bottom. The bay is all sand with no living coral and we did not see a single fish or anything else of interest. We were to more than make up for this later in the outer islands where we found waters teeming with every undersea thing that swims or crawls.

Aside from Magens there are no other anchorages on the north shore of St. Thomas that are of interest to yachtsmen. As the U. S. Pilot puts it: "Magens Bay is the only bight on the north shore of St. Thomas that is of any importance."

As already mentioned, the hills rising around the Magens Bay anchorage on three sides are high. Only a wind out of the north can get in there with any force behind it. At 10 A.M. when we weighed anchor there wasn't enough air to push a sailing canoe so we powered out. We passed Picara Point close enough to be unconcerned about Ornen Rock and soon picked up the breeze. We thought we would poke in

Tortola looms above as *Renegade* reaches toward Roadtown. Rufus was not only an excellent cook but could find his way around on deck balancing a tray of food in all weather.

between nearby Hans Lollik and Little Hans Lollik from the north and maybe try an anchorage there, so we continued powering to have a look. On the chart it seems to present a snug spot for a luncheon lay-over. But by the time we were there the wind was up to form and the big northerly swell was in action. This was ideal for sailing but not for anchoring. It looked cozy inside for scenery and on many days of the year would be fun to visit. We could see a white sand beach and seas breaking on the rocks beyond. We put the sails on and tacked offshore for several miles of first class sailing.

As many a sailor must have observed between Columbus' time and the present: "It's too bad the forty mile archipelago from St. Thomas to Anegada runs so east and west." To get to eastward it means a constant beat against the tradewind. Coming back it is a run all the way. If these hundred islands, cays and rocks had only been distributed north and south across the wind! But that would be all this and heaven too. We were not in a hurry and not concerned with proving that the shortest distance between two points is a straight line.

Our tack outward took us across the dotted line on the chart marking the "Approximate Boundary" between Great Britain and the U. S. Just after crossing the "boundary" Rufus hustled up on deck with a large tray of soup and sandwiches. I used to think Pullman dining-car waiters were the most adroit food purveyors in the world. But watching Rufus weave and slither across a heeling deck with heavy swells running as he balanced a tray on one hand was as fascinating as watching a high wire performance at the circus. As we came back in, leaving Little Tobago and Big Tobago to port, we picked up Carval Rock with the binoculars and by sheeting down thought we had a chance of making it on one tack. To the east beyond the two Tobagos (neither one to be confused with famed Tobago Island down near Trinidad) we could see Jost Van Dyke. This is one of the few of the British smaller islands which is inhabited. We went to anchor there later in the cruise. The Brasses, the Lolliks, all the islets and cays which we had passed are quite bare, uninhabited and uninviting. The same for Thatch Cay, Grass Cay, Mingo Cay, Lovango Cay and Congo Cay stringing out before us to starboard. In behind Thatch Cay, on St. Thomas proper, are several small stretches of white sand beach that are in the midst of the Virgin Island real estate subdivision scramble. Anchorages here are not good.

Two miles off Carval Rock we were headed by wind and current with no hope of rounding on the one tack. We closed within a hundred yards of Congo Cay and came about just as a series of black rain squalls came down from the east to meet us. In the next two hours we sailed through five of these squalls which gave us a lot of easting in a hurry. It was interesting to watch the squalls move toward us over the islands to windward, dumping their torrents of liquid contents in long shafts as they passed. At one time Jost Van Dyke was blacked-out so it wasn't there. But only for a few minutes. Then Jost was bright in the sunshine again and the Tobagos got it. Then the Tobagos were bright again and we picked up one. It's nice in this sort of thing to have new sails and perfect rigging and feel a well-designed vessel roar along under you at full hull speed.

Carval Rock received its name centuries ago when the caravels from Spain frequented these waters. From one angle it looks something like a high-pooped caravel hull with no sails showing. But after we had left it to enter Windward Passage we had a closer look and thought it most resembled an old fashioned cow-catcher type locomotive and coal car. We went for Hognest Point and leaving Durloe Cays to starboard we took off the headsails for the run downwind to Cruz Bay, St. John, where Government House is located.

CHAPTER II

ST. JOHN

As WE passed Hognest Point we entered a confusion of current and had to jibe twice before the wind took hold with authority and direction. Just inside Hognest Point was a particularly lovely short stretch of white beach with the prettiest house we had yet seen behind it. The house was of stone, low and set in a very luxurious growth of trees. This marked the beginning of the Rockefeller property at Caneel Bay Plantation. As we moved along we could see the several beaches picked by Laurance Rockefeller as the setting for his beach houses, dining room and lounge. We would visit Caneel Bay later. We wanted to proceed to Cruz, anchor, have a swim and look up some friends of friends who expected us.

Going into Cruz Bay one should favor the north shore and not get anywhere near the reefy shallows easily seen to starboard. After favoring the north side on entering, line up with the dock and anchor about two hundred yards off with a sandy bottom and twelve feet of depth.

As we anchored we were in the midst of quite a bit of activity. *The Chocolate Queen,* the rather worn-looking launch that shuttles people and mail back and forth to Redhook Bay on St. Thomas, came in. A Tortola sloop literally loaded to the gunwales—she was full of gravel and almost awash—came sailing to the dock. The *Sweet Gracie* a Tortola sloop which had been converted into a yacht of sorts brought a couple of people in from St. Croix. They later told us they had made the forty mile passage in six hours.

Looking out of Cruz Bay toward the west the horizon is a continuous chain of islands. The sloop in the center is so heavily laden with gravel she is almost awash.

It was 2 P.M. and very hot. We put up our awnings and swam for an hour before getting organized to go ashore.

The little Bay had not changed much to the eye since we had visited it two years before. In the interim a lot had happened to the island of St. John. It had become a full-fledged National Park. But Cruz Bay is out of bounds of the park and is still in the hands of many of the people who discovered it a dozen years before Mr. Rockefeller came along and bought up most of the island to present to the U. S. Along Gallows Point were the cottages of the Ellingtons. In from them were the cottages of the Fords. Behind the dock the few buildings of the little village looked almost the same as ever. On the low promontory to the left of the dock, old Government House stood with the Stars and Stripes fluttering over the ramparts. Behind Government House a couple of battered motorboats lay at the entrance to a small hurricane hole located there. On the hillside farther to the left a new and rather ambitious-looking home had gone up. It was of stone and had an open crescent porch facing us which looked like the shell of a band stand. All was quiet except for two brown pelicans who were after fish in the shallows near the reef and made tremendous splashes as they repeatedly crash-dived.

The little village at Cruz Bay is the only town on the island but has never been noted as a source of supply for yachts. We were therefore surprised to find quite a bit going on when we went ashore. There is a good little grocery store where we found plenty of canned goods, bacon, ham, fresh eggs and some vegetables for sale at reasonable prices. And at the emporium run by old St. John's hand Albert Sewer we found ice and plenty of it. Albert freezes it in big cakes in his Frigidaire and stows it in a deep freeze to be delivered over the counter at two cents a pound. Large letters over Albert's door proclaim:

SEWER'S CUT-RATE STORE
WEARING APPARELS

Albert Sewer is a tall friendly St. Johnian with a clipped mustachio and ready smile. His shop does not carry food, but for a little store only about twenty feet square has every kind of sundry from kitchen utensils

Renegade is anchored farthest out, opposite the Ellington cottages at Cruz Bay. Government House is on the end of the peninsula in the foreground. It dates back to the days of Danish rule.

Photo by Eunice Boardman

Albert Sewer learned dress designing in New York and now his creations are marketed in the Leeward Islands as well as the Virgins. Here he greets the author on St. John.

to jewelry. The surprising part of his operation is a small annex built on the back where several women operate sewing machines. Albert went to New York for training in the garment district and now is the Christian Dior of the outer islands. He designs all kinds of dresses and fancy blouses and shorts for women and personally sells his creations as far south as St. Kitts. He imports his fabrics from New York and even produces wedding gowns from his own designs. Hazel and Eunice tried on some Sewer-designed Bermuda shorts and bought two pairs each. The emporium handles very little apparel for men. Albert frankly explains why he specializes in women's things rather than men's,

"The man, he never has money for hisself. He always have two women to buy for, his wife an his lady frien'. So I concentrates only on the female market an' sell twice as much stuff as otherwise."

Albert has great hopes for the future of Cruz Bay and showed us an elaborate "Prospectus of the St. John Development Corporation—owned by the People of St. John."

The four incorporators of the new scheme are Mr. Theovald Moorhead (a Senator and proprietor of Mooie's Bar and Pool Room), Ex-Senator Julius E. Spruave, Sr., Ronald A. Morrisette (a continental who owns the band-stand house on the hill) and Albert Sewer.

The Prospectus quotes Senator (Mooie) Moorehead thus: "I ask you to consider a very disturbing fact. The tourist industry in the West Indies is growing tremendously. But in all the West Indies there is not a single island where the native people have a hand in the industry to any important degree. Tourism is usually in the hands of a few outsiders who have the initiative, the experience and the money to invest. The island people must stand aside."

The Prospectus goes on: "Well, on St. John you don't have to stand aside. You can exercise the same intelligence that other people do—and make the same kind of profits—in the big tourist industry that is starting on this island."

The incorporators propose that the new corporation sell stock to native investors at $1.00 a share and thereby raise $100,000 over the next two years to put up a restaurant, hotel, boat yard, information center, handicraft center and an expanded boat service to St. Thomas.

Here, in the words of the islanders, is a summation of their position, retaining as they do a toe-hold of a few acres at the entrance to the new National Park area.

"St. John is at the very beginning of an unusually intense period of development. Touristically the island has just recently been discovered. Three years ago few continental Americans had any but the vaguest idea of the existence of the Virgin Islands; fewer still had ever heard of St. John.

"Now St. John is probably the most widely publicized island this side of Hawaii. The discovery of St. John and its development as a tourist haven was inevitable in this expanding tourist age. But it has been greatly accelerated by the elaborate building program at Caneel Bay [the Rockefeller establishment] which has given this island the impetus of an unsurpassed resort, and by the establishment of the Virgin Islands National Park.

"A National Park inevitably promotes increases in tourist traffic. In the U. S. people interested in sure business opportunities compete fiercely for concessions in the parks, or for locations close to park boundaries because they know that with thousands of visitors wanting food, hotels, camping grounds, bus and taxi tours and souvenirs there is a great deal of money to be made in providing these services."

In the closing paragraph the Prospectus has a few soothing words for the more timid prospective investor. "Meanwhile, of course, this corporation should be paying at least 10% in dividends each year . . . And, in a good corporation your stock is easily sold if for any reason you have to sell it. Thus, an investor always has something to fall back on in an emergency like sickness. It is something a man might never have if he had not saved his money in this way. It can be seen that this is just about the only way to make money without working for it. Your savings do the work."

It would certainly be poetic justice if this "Corporation of The People," 95% of the stockholders being descendants of slaves who worked the old cane plantations, achieved its aims. We wished them well.

Another interesting native personality of Cruz Bay is Andromeda Keating. A few steps from the dock is the small gray house with white louvres where she takes in a few paying guests at reasonable rates. The place is unpretentious and a bit reminiscent of a stage set for Maugham's "Rain." Miss Andromeda is noted for her creole cooking and when we dropped by to see her outside her little cook shack at the rear she was overseeing the broiling of lobsters over a couple of native charcoal braziers. Miss Andromeda is a large woman with a pretty, modest smile. Her only hobby besides cooking is raising peacocks. To come upon her flock of seven of these birds pecking and preening around the cook shack door is a startling experience. She inherited a cock and hen from her mother and raised the five younger birds from the eggs. She has given them all Biblical names: Paul, John, Joseph, Isaiah, Thomas, James and Matthew. Miss Andromeda says the birds are not just beautiful and dumb. Each will answer to its name when called. They are definitely not being raised to eat, she claims.

One rather sad note: Miss Andromeda took us into a new little cement dining room she had just built next to the cook house. It had tables and chairs of stainless steel and formica and looked exactly like the inside of one of those aluminum diners along the Boston Post Road. Another surrender of the quaint and primitive to "modernize" for what she believes will attract the rich continentals.

When we walked around the shore road to contact Marnie and Tom Ford, the couple we were supposed to look up, we found them swimming off their beach. They had three cottages a short walk from the dock and rented two of them while living in the third. The Fords had come to the island from Mansfield, Ohio, where he had a successful insurance business. They were not trying to run away from any particular problems. They were just sick of the northern weather and the tensions of daily U.S. life in general. They had saved their money and resolved not to touch any of the principal but to live off the interest. They did not own their cottages but leased them. By renting the two (at $200.00 per week in the season), they lived well in the third. They traveled each year either to the States or Europe and wouldn't trade the life they led for anything. They had just returned from two months in Scandinavia.

The Fords took us on what was up to then the most memorable jeep ride we had ever had. I say "up to then" because some weeks later we had rides that almost equalled it on the back roads of St. Thomas and St. Croix. Tom at fifty-five years of age drove a jeep the way a cowboy rides the range and over just as wild territory. He took us over roads that were roughly bull-dozed through the bush straight up in the air and then down boulder-strewn trails that all but jounced us through the top. Marnie, an exceptionally beautiful and feminine blonde, insisted on sitting in the rear seat. She wanted Hazel, Eunice and me in the front and middle seats so we could hear Tom above the bang and clatter of the ride. We kept looking back to see if she was still with us.

Island people, we have found, can be as tight-lipped as Vermonters if they don't know you and don't know whether they are going to like you if they do know you. When you speak the same language they open up with a charming frankness, guilelessness, and independence of thought that is in refreshing contrast to the blasé cynical sophistication of too many self-satisfied continentals.

As we drove for two hours over every road and goat trail, through every bog and gravel pit on the island, Tom responded to all our queries with humor and enthusiasm.

On driving tourists around: "If they know something about St. John and are sincerely interested I love to drive people around. But when they ask dumb questions and don't seem to know whether the island is part of Jamaica, Haiti or Florida I blow my top. We had some people here the other day who said they hoped Rockefeller would build a bridge over to St. Thomas."

On photographers: "Some of those characters from the picture mag-azines should be put in a rocket and shot to the moon. They come in here as though they were doing us a great favor to recognize our quaint little island. They expect everything for free from hotel accommoda-tions to food and drink, and keep little notebooks of their expense accounts besides."

On Rockefeller: "Mr. Rockefeller is a fine man and had of course the noblest of intentions when he bought up most of this island to give to the U. S. for a National Park. But he is involved in so many things that he personally cannot keep track of what is going on. Families who have lived happily here for generations succumb to the fabulous prices Rockefeller lieutenants offer, sell out, fall out with each other and don't know where to go or what to do."

[33]

St. John has not had many people on it since slave days. Now about seven hundred negroes and one hundred whites make up the population. About half the whites are working for the Rockefeller operation. A half dozen Americans still retain winter homes on St. John. The Rockefeller interests are buying these as they gradually come on the market. Some will be used for Park Ranger accommodations, some for more guest houses. Some are already disintegrating from non-use. One or two are mansions that are useless for anything but a retired millionaire who can afford to keep an army of retainers. These mansions the jungle will claim. We didn't visit Caneel Bay Plantation, the Rockefeller Hotel, because we planned to anchor there later.

We did drive beyond beautiful Trunk Bay beach and see the little hotel on the bluff that had been operated by the Boulon family for the past thirty years. This we were told, was about to be dismantled and turned over to the Park, having been acquired by the Rockefeller interests. This rather primitively run establishment was long famous for its seclusion and West Indian cooking. It was a favorite haunt of such literary lights as John Dos Pasos and John Gunther. Dos Pasos met and wooed his second wife there. An anecdote about Gunther's last visit to Trunk Bay still persists. The author arrived by sea before the new road was bulldozed and as his luggage was transferred to a dinghy he refused to let anyone carry a bulging briefcase which was full of his latest *Inside Africa* notes. He fell into the water, of course, only to surface splutteringly as a wag yelled "Trunk Bay is now inside Gunther." The notes were rescued and duly dried out.

From the top heights of St. John we saw more of what we had seen atop St. Thomas. But St. John being so sparsely settled offered the greater feeling of enjoying the as-yet unspoiled. True, the creation of the park guarantees that the rolling hills of St. John will never be dotted with homesteads. But if the vision of bus loads and boat loads of thousands of visiting tourists materializes the roads and surrounding tranquil waters will one day buzz with activity.

On the drive back to Cruz Bay, Tom drove the jeep to the edge of a secluded, small and perfectly tree-shaded white sand bathing beach. This is the beach to which visitors are driven by the organized tours of the Park which originate on St. Thomas. Groups are brought over by boat to Cruz Bay and there they are jeeped to points of interest on the island for a fee that includes box lunches and a swim at this particular beach. But when they ask "Where do we change our clothes?" they are told to step into the bushes. Some people feel this is downright unhandy, if not rather too clubby in a mixed group of strangers. Tom is good friends with the Park rangers and offered to donate the erection of a small changing shed in the bush if the Park Service would furnish wood and nails. This was turned down by officialdom in Washington as not within their appropriation. Instead they sent out some refuse cans which cost $20.00 apiece and so far have not been needed. Some smart desk man also sent out some neatly printed signs to be put up on this otherwise unspoilt and deserted beach. We read one which had been cemented into the center of the beach on an iron stand:

NOTICE

NATIONAL PARK SERVICE

HUNTING PROHIBITED

Warning is hereby given to all persons that it is unlawful to hunt, trap, carry unsealed firearms, etc. It is also prohibited to: camp or light fires except at designated camp grounds or to permit dogs to run at large in the Park. Persons violating any of the above will be subject to a fine of $500 or six months in prison.

Since there was nothing to hunt on the island and nothing to attract dogs to this far-away and inaccessible spot these signs could have been laughed of by the natives as merely silly. But the signs were eyesores and as such should have been destroyed by any civic-minded St. Johnian, except for the P.S. on the bottom of each sign warning more fines and imprisonment if the signs were defaced or destroyed. Tom remarked to us that such policing was as ridiculous as if someone put a barbed wire fence around the peak of Mt. Everest.

One of the great charms of cruising, as everyone knows, is that you go when and where you please—you operate completely by whim. The morning we sailed out of Cruz Bay we decided to start counter-clockwise around St. John and anchor in Reef Bay on the southern

Photo by Sam Falk

Ronald Morrisette of Cruz Bay inspects the ancient Carib carvings above the reflecting pool near Reef Bay on the south shore of St. John. Note comic strip head in center.

Photo by Ed. Hagan

A friend from Yacht Haven made this picture of *Renegade* about to anchor in Francis Bay, St. John. The European custom of flying the ensign while under sail is V. I. practice.

shore. Here we planned to run the dinghy onto the beach and try to find the old Carib carvings which are in the bush a half hour's walk inshore. We knew that if the wind was coming much from the south there would be a heavy swell running against us as we approached open sea, so as a preliminary precaution we had hauled the dinghy aboard and made everything fast on deck and below.

It was fortunate everything was well-secured for after we left Steven Cay to starboard and got out to where Pillsbury Sound meets the Caribbean, *Renegade* was soon bucking some very heavy and confused seas. It had been blowing strong from south of east all night and here, where hundreds of miles of the Caribbean funnels into Pillsbury, the buildup can on occasion amount to something. The sailing was fine and exhilarating but we could soon see that on this day there would not be a chance of landing a dinghy at the head of Reef Bay, a very exposed piece of lee shore with the wind where it was. In other words it was a great day for sailing but there was too much surf piling up for attempting landings on the south shore of St. John except in places we didn't want to go.

We came about and had a broad reach back to our starting point, sailed past Caneel and Hognest Point again and, leaving well-buoyed Johnson Reef to starboard, went in to have a look at Francis Bay. Here the wind was right in our eye and we had to take off the sails and power. This is another beautiful bay dotted with sandy beaches and containing plenty of good overnight anchorages easily spotted near the steep-to shore. The PILOT says of Francis Bay: ". . . good anchorage in 9 fathoms, sandy bottom."

Next we passed through Fungi Passage between the high bluffs of Whistling Cay and Mary Point. We agreed with the PILOT DIRECTIONS which say of tight little Fungi Passage: "It has a charted depth of 21 feet but on account of the baffling winds from the adjacent high land, it is not easily navigated by sailing vessels."

Here a word should be said about the use of auxiliary power in these islands. We all know the purists who sail in and out of everywhere and pride themselves on clever navigation even at night in new places without recourse to motor. There are almost none of these yachtsmen in Virgin Island waters today. I queried every sailor I met about this

Looking northeast across Trunk Bay on St. John, the Boulon houses are above the end of the beach. Above them is Fungi Passage leading past Mary Point into The Narrows.

noble practice and found no old hand in the area who would go along with it. Of course, native sailors with their shoal-draft hulls continue to navigate everywhere without power. And plenty of them regularly go aground. But they can easily get off and they can row themselves out of trouble in places where a heavy keel yacht is helpless.

One such "wind-only" purist who with his wife had sailed his forty foot schooner all around the Mediterranean and across the Atlantic to base in the Virgin Islands said this: "A yacht without power may go a season here or even two seasons and with care and luck never get into trouble. I did this very thing but had so many close calls I decided I was depending more on luck than skill. After twenty-five years of purist sailing I at last broke down and put a motor in my boat. Sure, there are very few hidden dangers here. This is truly a sailing paradise with good anchorages everywhere and steep-to shores and easily seen hazards. But if the wind dies when you are in a tight place with a four knot current running what do you do next?"

On Whistling Cay, as we moved on into The Narrows, we saw the remains of a small and ancient structure on the beach facing Francis Bay. It was roofless but its thick walls of old masonry were standing intact. We had been told that this was a sentry post where the early Danish planters kept armed lookouts to intercept slaves attempting to run away from St. John and find asylum in the British settlement on the West End of Tortola.

When we entered The Narrows we thought again of our friends the purists. The wind was very light and baffling and were we not under power the current was running westerly strong enough to deposit us on the rocky shore of Whistling Cay in a hurry. Query: How did the caravels of ancient days manage? Answer: Plenty went to the bottom. Also they never attempted a west to east passage here. Coming from east to west they anchored at Tortola's West End if conditions were uncertain, and waited for favorable wind and current before attempting to shoot The Narrows.

The wind came strong again and straight at us as we drew abeam of Little Thatch Isle. An American was building a bungalow development on Little Thatch and we tooted our horn and got an answering hail from shore as we passed. We planned to stop in for a call on our way back from the outer islands. On our right hand on the St. John shore we had noted an old sugar mill prominent above the beach of another beautiful bay, Leinster. (It is impossible to think of another adjective for these bays—they are all beautiful.) The easternmost part of Leinster Bay is a bay within a bay. This is called Watermelon Bay and according to the *Pilot Directions*: "it is partially protected by Watermelon Cay, 30 feet high lying 250 yards westward of Leinster Point. The cay is bold and is separated from St. John by a channel 200 yards wide carrying 2 fathoms of water. Vessels may anchor under the cay about 200 yards from shore."

Beyond Little Thatch we gained sea room and picked up the well-known breeze. It was a great relief to be bowling along again under sail. In four tacks we were off Pelican Islet and The Indians, and headed for the Bight of Norman. In the tacks toward Tortola we noted what an overpowering mass this biggest of the British Virgins is. It truly dwarfs everything else in sight.

Pelican Islet should have been called Pelican Rock. It is a small bare bluff not two hundred feet high and fits the phrase "for the birds." About two hundred yards to westward of Pelican are The Indians, four pinnacles of stone close together and rising about fifty feet above the sea. They must have been so-named because they are in close file, Indian fashion. To by-pass Ringdove Rock, an unmarked hazard with two fathoms over it, we went for Treasure Point, the southern entrance to The Bight.

Chapter III

NORMAN ISLAND

WE WERE at anchor in the Bight of Norman Island, described in the U. S. PILOT DIRECTIONS as an "Excellent anchorage. And although open to the westward St. John Island prevents any sea from setting in, and the holding ground is good." The PILOT also says that the wind in the lee of Norman is at times so baffling that sailing vessels may have to "anchor at the entrance and warp in."

We found the wind light and baffling at the entrance, but thanks to *Renegade*'s trusty diesel we did not have to warp in. We went to within a hundred yards of the inner shore and anchored in three fathoms.

There is something about Norman Island that lingers with you once you have anchored in the Bight. We visited Norman twice and have felt the pull of the place ever since. There's no way to explain it but that the island has a special brand of magic that gets to you. At a glance Norman looks like any of twenty-five other uninhabited islands of its size in the Virgins. Perhaps it is the association with pirate lore. Pirates really were there and pirate treasure really has been found there. About fifty years ago a chest loaded with Spanish gold and jewels was found on a ledge in one of the water caves outside Treasure Point. Perhaps it is the isolated tranquillity of the Bight. Once again we were in a bay that seemed sealed off like a mountain lake. But unlike the dead waters of Magens we were now in a place vibrant with action. Fifty pelicans and as many boobies were diving in the shallows all around us.

This is how the cave entrances outside Treasure Point at Norman look from the sea. The cave at the left is the deepest one. It is supposed to be the treasure cave.

We could look anywhere off the deck and see schools of fingerlings moving in glittering masses. Close by and far off thousands broke the surface in waves as they were fed upon with saber slashes from underneath. Every so often one of the predators broke the surface in an arc of such speed the eye had to be quick to follow.

"And now for the caves," said Eunice.

We loaded the dinghy with snorkels, spear guns, swim fins, an anchor and a couple of inflated mattresses with holes in the ends for viewing through glass face masks. There was so much gear that there was barely room for two of us in the dinghy. Hazel stayed behind confessing that she was not particularly cave-minded. *Skipperkey* made a five foot leap and joined us just as we got the outboard going and started off.

The three caves, just outside Treasure Point, are not hard to find. But the one that looks most like a cave goes in only a few feet. Cave number one, nearest the Point is the largest and has an entrance not visible from the sea. We rowed into a notch on the rocky shore then turned right for the entrance. At this juncture I was quite ready to confess that I was not too cave-minded myself.

"Hey, it's dark as the inside of a cow in there," I said.

"And wouldn't you know it. We forgot the flashlights," said Eunice. "We ought to have a check list."

"Well, that's too bad. But we can come back another time." I tried to sound disappointed.

"Oh, I've been in there before. I think we can manage it without a light."

So I started rowing. Just inside the entrance the oars had about four inches of clearance. It was light enough here to see swarms of fish herding below us among the coral heads as the water shallowed to about a fathom. We had a good ten feet of headroom to the dripping top of the grotto above us, but as the surge of the sea from outside suddenly rose under us I found myself wishing I had worn a crash helmet. Soon the oars wouldn't clear and we just had room to paddle. A few yards farther in, the cave took a turn and we were in total darkness. I thought I remembered an etching by Gustave Doré depicting the Gates of Hell. I said "Wow."

Eunice maneuvers the dinghy to enter Treasure cave while *Skipperkey* barks. There is little tide to worry about here but sometimes a dangerous swell builds up making entry impossible.

Eunice mistook my remark for a pleased reaction and said, "It *is* terrific, isn't it?"

But the things most trying on the nerves were yet to come. The air was suddenly in motion overhead with the whir of a thousand wings. *Skipperkey*, who had been absolutely quiet up to this time, now uttered a low whine. "Bats," said Eunice matter-of-factly. Then the bats started to squeek, rodents that they are, and soon the vaulted tomb-like grotto echoed with their mouse-like voices.

Now I was surprised to find that some of my vision was coming back. It was the sudden contrast from the tropic sun outside which had made the cave seem so pitch dark at first. We were at the cave's end, about one hundred feet in, yet enough light was transmitted through the water so one could just barely make out where water and walls met.

"Now put on your mask and go over the side and I'll tow you out."

"What was that again?"

"I said put on your mask and go over the side and I'll tow you out. You'll get a thrill you'll never forget."

"I've already had a thrill I'll never forget."

I hated to be chicken about it. I wondered how many of my sea-going friends would have done otherwise. But I didn't have long to sit and wonder.

"Here goes!" Splash.

I was suddenly alone in the boat with *Skipperkey*. Needless to say I got us out into the daylight in a hurry. As the dinghy emerged from the cave Eunice grabbed the gunwale and tossed a five pound lobster in beside me. She had spotted his antenna under a coral head near the entrance and had shot him between the eyes with her spear gun.

It has been argued that the clawless lobster of the Caribbean is not a lobster at all, but a langouste, a kind of big crayfish. I have been corrected off and on by Yankee friends who insist that only the be-clawed lobster of Maine is a true lobster. Yet thousands of pounds of Caribbean "crayfish" are shipped weekly to smart hotels in the tourist belt where lobster salads and lobster cocktails enjoy top billing on the menus. The toothsome crustaceans abound in the coral reefs of almost every one of these tropical islands and can be picked up with little effort. When natives offer them for sale in the out islands the price is

Skipperkey rode the stern of the dinghy as we made our exit of Treasure Cave. To the left of her silhouette Eunice is busy snorkeling. Just inside the entrance she speared a five pound lobster.

around 15 cents per pound. Often natives offer to trade them for an old shirt or pair of shorts. We adjusted our vocabulary to fit this barter system by forgetting poundage and speaking in terms of half-shirt lobsters, one-shirt lobsters, or two-shirt lobsters, depending as much on the condition of the shirt as the weight of the lobster.

Eunice has always claimed she cannot swim. She says that without breathing equipment and fins she would go down to the bottom and not come up. We never had a chance to put this to the test for whenever she was in the water (which was a great deal of the time) she wore snorkeling gear. If she cannot swim it is about the only athletic challenge she ever by-passed. She excelled in skiing, tennis and golf until a bad airplane accident ruled out active competitive sport for her. She was a pilot in the air-ferry command during the war and was delivering a beat-up twin engined transport for repairs when both engines failed and she made a crash landing. After months of hospitalization and bone surgery she was released looking as pert and alive as ever but with very much weakened leg bones. This was when she turned to sailing.

Outside the cave we anchored the dinghy and, with *Skipperkey* scolding us with sharp barks from the bow, we swam along a few yards over a coral garden abounding in tropical fish of every color and design. We soon came to another cave, this one with a shallow entrance and T-shaped inside with short passages to right and left. Eunice, of course, went right in and I decided there was nothing for it but to follow. The place was well-lighted from the sun outside and through our face glasses we were treated to an underwater scene of amazing color. There were splotches and blobs of bright purple, orange, reds and greens on the rocks below us that looked as though an artist had squeezed oil paints fresh from their tubes everywhere. The water was only waist deep and when we stood up the walls around us looked like a miniature cathedral with all the colors of the Grand Canyon at sunset. An ancient has said "we fear most those things unseen." In this second cave with the glow from the water illuminating all of it in a soft light, even the bats were interesting as they fluttered back and forth overhead and hung upside down in rows along the arched ceiling.

By the time we had regained the dinghy I was ready to brave the blackness of cave number one again. While Eunice looked further for lobster outside I swam slowly all the way in and out again. Halfway out

I noticed a spur which branched off to the left and thought what a start it would give one to branch off by mistake. Next day we took Hazel along and flashlights and rowed into this spur to find that it did not proceed very far. We wondered if this was the spot where the treasure was found.

Norman Island was named for a pirate skipper who had a one-man kingdom on the island and for many years preyed upon the shipping that passed through Sir Francis Drake Channel. For two hundred years the Norman treasure legend had persisted, but it was not until just after the turn of the last century that an impoverished Virgin Islander named Creque made a systematic search of the caves and found the treasure chest previously mentioned. The well-heeled Creque family are prominent merchants in St. Thomas to this day.

In the book LAGOONED IN THE VIRGIN ISLANDS, published by Routledge and Sons of London, author H. B. Eadie appears to have done considerable research on Norman Island. This account refers to a letter dated December 22, 1750, in which reference is made to the "troublesome Spaniards infesting the seas around the Virgin Islands and recovering part of the loot from the caravel *Nuestra Senora* which had been buried at Norman Island . . ." Old records are quoted to show that the *Nuestra Senora* was driven ashore in a storm August 18, 1750, on the coast of North Carolina. At the time she was carrying the President of Santo Domingo and almost half a million dollars in gold and silver plate. After the grounding the President procured another vessel, loaded it with the treasure and started south, only to be hijacked by pirates who took the loot to Norman Island and buried it there.

Some time after the Spaniards and their guard ships had swooped down on Norman Island and killed the pirate captain and his followers, a group of Englishmen formed a Norman's Island Treasure Company and a great deal of gun powder was wasted blasting all over the place. Some of these holes can be seen today.

Of the many treasure stories about these islands, all seem to go back so many years as to be slightly legendary. As recently as February, 1953, however, *Travel Magazine* reported in an article called "I Lifted Treasure from the Caribbean," by Lieut. Harry E. Rieseberg, that the author found the submerged wreck of the Spanish Galleon *El Capitan* some eighty-five miles north of Nassau and recovered a large assortment of gold bars, and gold Aztec figurines. The locale "eighty-five miles north of Nassau" is not exactly in the Caribbean but near enough I suppose for purposes of the article. Altogether $100,000 worth of treasure was brought up from the *El Capitan* which had lain on the bottom in sixteen fathoms for almost two and a half centuries. Lieut. Rieseberg had found it necessary to use dynamite to disintegrate the ship and no doubt because of this a considerable portion of her cargo was lost in the explosion.

The afternoon of our second day at Norman, Hazel, Eunice and I went snorkeling close inshore to a small reef where the pelicans were especially busy. If I hadn't had two witnesses I would doubt forever what I saw. A few feet offshore in about six feet of water I was swimming slowly through a school of small fish and came out the other side to meet up with two tarpon face to face. Tarpon have been recorded as long as eight feet and weighing up to three hundred fifty pounds. This pair were at least two hundred pounds each and looked as large as anything I hope to see underwater. They didn't make a move and neither did I. I snorted through my snorkel, a prearranged signal to say I had sighted something. In a couple of minutes Eunice and Hazel joined me and the tarpons still hung motionless like fish mounted in an exhibit at the Museum of Natural History. We looked at the fish and they at us for almost five minutes during this impasse. We noticed that one had part of its tail fin missing. One of our fish books had said there is no more thrilling sight underwater than to come upon a good sized specimen of His Majesty The Tarpon. With this statement I heartily agree but we were due for an anticlimax. Eunice suddenly waved her spear gun around to the rear and there, stretching across our line of retreat, was a six foot barracuda. The two tarpon at this point glided off. The barracuda turned toward us and stared.

Our fish book had said the West Indian or Great Barracuda is the species thoroughly established as being dangerous to bathers. "This is fact and not open to question in the sense that some shark records are," according to the book.

In another of our books FLORIDA FISH AND FISHING by the well-known angler Phil Francis, it is flatly stated that the barracuda is harmless to man.

"The barracuda is popularly supposed to be a savage incautious sea tiger that strikes viciously at anything moving in the water, but this is just another misconception about him. Actually the barracuda is an even-tempered easy-going fish neither given to reckless and gluttonous feeding nor susceptible to teasing.

"The barracuda's curious nature is probably at least partly responsible for his reputation as a threat to human life. He does seem to find human swimmers intensely fascinating and it takes a steel-nerved stoic to meet a 'cuda face to face in the water without getting panicky. If you retreat he'll follow you but not with any idea of attacking. He just can't figure you out, yet his curiosity compels him to try. If you move slowly toward him he'll back off and keep his distance; if you make a quick move in his direction he'll scram."

Our 'cuda must have been a Florida 'cuda for he stared at us a couple of seconds and scrammed. Then we scrammed, but as we did so came cheek by jowl upon the two tarpon again. These were unquestionably the same pair. One had part of its tail fin chewed off.

The cocktail hour was naturally enough given over to fish talk. Author Francis having given us such a good steer in dealing with barracudas we turned to his book and looked up the chapters on tarpon. According to Francis, who has boated as many tarpon as any other angler of our time, this enormously powerful fish is the fightingest, leapingest, most majestic, graceful game fish in the world. Mr. Francis cites a 115 pound tarpon that towed a fisherman's boat around fourteen and a half hours before being brought to gaff.

Zane Grey in his TALES OF SOUTHERN RIVERS tells how a two hundred pound tarpon towed a fisherman's dinghy for six hours before being landed.

Eunice had a fitting anecdote to contribute at this point. She said she had seen big tarpon at the same place in Norman Bight before. Last trip through the islands she had some friends aboard who were crazy about fishing and had brought loads of expensive rods and lures down from New York but had not caught a thing. She swam them to the shallows where we had been and promised them some excitement. She tied four self-inflating life jackets to her spear gun and resolved to try a shot at a tarpon figuring that when the fish was harpooned he would leave like a shot, but the life jackets would bring him to the surface somewhere where he might be found. A seven foot tarpon turned up as by appointment. With her tense gallery watching she maneuvered to the rear quarter of the fish to allow the spear to get in under his scales. So sure was she of the shot that as she fired she also triggered the self-inflating jackets. The tension inside the face masks was now at fever pitch. "Poing" went the spear. And it bounced off the hide of the tarpon like a straw hitting an elephant. The big fish then glided slowly away as if to say "what fools these mortals be." The self-inflating life jackets were the expendable type that are no good after having been once blown up. They represented a loss of $10.00.

The scales on a tarpon are the biggest and toughest armor of any fish. On big fish the scales are three inches across and often used to make jewelry novelties.

The same American couple who had such bad luck fishing in the Virgin Islands were slightly victimized by an attempt by Felix to be helpful. One late afternoon at Norman, after the anglers had spent all day trolling, casting, and line fishing, using every lure and rod combination imaginable, Felix approached the dejected pair in the cockpit and said "Maybe I try something?"

They laughingly gave the young colored boy a rod and box of tackle and he took the dinghy and was off. He disappeared around Treasure Point and was back in half an hour with a dozen fine fish flapping around in the bottom of the boat. He had jacks, parrot fish and several beautiful specimens of snapper.

The fishermen were appalled and very much chagrined.

"These natives," said the man, "know all the tricks of black magic but why don't they pass a little of this know-how on to us. After all we didn't come one thousand five hundred miles just to be humiliated." His wife agreed and tried to wheedle some information out of Felix. But Felix couldn't explain. He was polite enough but merely said "I jes' humbug de fish."

Felix had sincerely tried to be helpful. But Eunice knew before cornering him alone what had happened. He had robbed a fish trap. She made him take the dinghy and go back to the trap, raise it and tie a bottle of rum in it for the hapless Tortola native who would visit his pilfered trap next evening.

CHAPTER IV

PETER ISLAND

Our next landfall (landfall is hardly the term for islands in sight of each other) was nearby Peter Island where we anchored in Little Harbor close up to a sandy beach at the head of the bay. Peter Island is almost twice as large as Norman, is shaped like an elbow, and at its highest point rises five hundred feet above the sea.

Above Little Harbor was a single white house which a look through our glasses proved to be shuttered at the time. The house had been originally erected by an eccentric Englishman, one Sir Brundel Bruce, who sometimes appeared in St. Thomas wearing the tunic, baggy pants and short boots of a Russian dancer. He also carried a shepherd's staff and sported a monocle. The Bruce property had later been purchased by Mr. Percy Chubb II a commodore of the New York Yacht Club.

Peter Island has three other good anchorages on its north shore, Great Harbor, Sprat Harbor and Deadman Bay. We were told that a Norwegian Shipping magnate had recently purchased some five hundred acres around Sprat Bay and a large hotel and marina complex was planned. (See Chapter XVII)

Great Harbor is twice as large as Little Harbor and is described in the Pilot Book thus: "A snug little bight on the northern shore of Peter Island, about 0.5 miles in extent and may be entered without any difficulty at any time. It has deep water close up to the shore and the holding ground is excellent. The harbor is open to the northwestward but is rather smooth as it is sheltered from that direction by Tortola." While we were swimming we watched a pair of fishermen come to the mouth of the bay and execute a dazzling maneuver. They were sailing one of the typical Tortola sloops, about thirty feet overall, and moving with great speed on a broad reach. They didn't bother to come up into the wind as they approached the markers of a fish trap but reached over and pulled the float inboard and let the boat come up by herself. This required not only quick timing but great strength. Without lowering sail they pulled up the big basket trap at the end of its long line, emptied its contents, baited and dropped it again and were off to Norman. Quite an exhibition for descendants of a people supposed to be languid and lazy forest dwellers. We wondered if these were the fellows who had found the present Eunice left for them outside Treasure Point.

DEAD MAN'S CHEST

We next sailed around to Dead Man's Chest and anchored in the bay of that name on Peter. The charts and PILOT BOOK call this Dead Chest but since it is the inspiration for Robert Louis Stevenson's "Fifteen Men on Dead Man's Chest" it is a shame to condense the term. In my youth I had it "Fifteen men on a dead man's chest" and used to try to figure out how fifteen pirates might arrange themselves for standing room on the breast of a corpse. In my imagination I pictured a sort of acrobatic troupe with three anchor-men actually on the cadaver and twelve more balancing on their heads and shoulders. Then in later years I figured that the men might possibly be doing their act on the *sea chest* of a dead man. This seemed more reasonable, allowing for a sea chest large enough for five anchor-men at the bottom. When I finally learned the true story, that old buccaneer Edward Teach had marooned fifteen men, one bottle of rum and a cutlass on this very rock called Dead Man's Chest, I decided that the cay must have some outstanding characteristic worth noting.

But Dead Chest is just another small and very ordinary looking rock jutting a couple of hundred feet out of the sea. It sits about half a mile off the northeastern end of Peter Island and it would not be too difficult a swim either way for a really energetic pirate. If you want to explore Dead Man's Chest you can find a fair anchorage off its northwest tip.

The swimming off Dead Chest beach (Peter Island) where we anchored was excellent. This is one of the few beaches in the Virgins that is palm-shaded like the pictures on travel brochures. We found good snorkeling off the rocks at either end of the beach and Eunice shot a baby stingray which made a delicious salad. The meaty part of the small ray is white, tender and tastes a bit like crab flakes. It should be boiled about thirty minutes, then iced. Larger rays are tough and have a strong oily flavor.

SALT ISLAND

The next islet of interest to the eastward is Salt, only a mile in length but inhabited by a hardy colony of natives who make salt in the ponds there, just as their ancestors did two hundred years ago. The little settlement under a few palms looked quite picturesque as we anchored a hundred yards from shore in the bight at the western end of the island. A native sloop rode at anchor near us. Several boats were hauled up on the beach where some nets were drying.

But when we went ashore we found a very impoverished-looking community. The shacks were of old boards and pieces of rusty tin and were papered on the inside with old newspapers. We were greeted by a pretty young woman as we passed one shack, and as we talked to her we had a glimpse of the interior. Her place was a bit more elaborate than the others. It was papered with advertising pages from *Life* in full color. On a box in a corner of the room a radio was going and the smooth voice of an M. C. was saying "and now we want to send special birthday congratulations to Mrs. Maria Eduardo of San Juan—and always remember that enchantment is yours at the Caribe Hilton, gem of the Caribbean."

The young woman took us fifty yards behind her house and pointed out one of the salt ponds to us. There are three on the island, about

[55]

We were surprised to happen upon this brooding lion jutting out from shore near our anchorage at Salt Island. He seemed an appropriate symbol for the British Virgins.

two thousand bags of salt being shipped out each season at $2.00 a bag.

An old, old man dressed in white dungarees and a tattered black coat sat on the rail of a beached boat. He was leaning on a cane propped in the sand between his knees. When we approached him he struggled rustily to his feet and tipped his frayed hat to Hazel. We motioned him to sit down and we sat on the edge of a canoe opposite to him. We had read that the *Rhone*, a Royal Mail Liner, had foundered on the shore of Salt Island in the hurricane of October 29, 1867. This gale was one of the more memorable ones for it had been accompanied by a tidal wave which caused extra damage throughout the islands. The old man looked ancient enough to know something, at least by hearsay, about the *Rhone* disaster.

"You have a big ship sink here long time ago?" I asked.

"Yessuh de wreck is on de sout' side," he pointed his stick across the salt pond. "My faddah he help bury some ob de corpses here. Many, many, many peoples drownded."

The *Rhone* was propelled by steam as well as sail and had been caught while running down Drake Channel for St. Thomas on her maiden voyage from England to the West Indies. As gale force winds struck her from the southeast she first sought shelter in Peter Island's Great Harbour. Then the wind had moved around to the north and to escape being trapped against a lee shore she tried to steam out and run for the open sea through Salt Island Passage. Here her engines proved futile against the wind and she smashed onto Salt Island's rocky shore to slide back into the sea and go down in ten fathoms. Her submerged hulk can be viewed today when the water is calm. But on the day of our call heavy seas were breaking on the south shore, and although the old man remarked "Plenty big fish in de wreck" it would have been hopeless trying to see anything.

On leaving the anchorage at Salt we were intrigued by an odd formation of rocks astride the eastern point containing the bay. From the angle we were headed the rocks looked exactly like a large sculptured lion couchánt. As we moved in closer the head of the beast looked very much the British lion. Its forepaws were extended in classical fashion but its rear was a bit caricatured like the rear of a Thurber dog about to spring. We made some pictures and looked in our books to see if we were viewing a known landmark. But the lion guarding Salt has apparently gone unnoted up to now.

We had a broad reach crossing from Salt Island to the great harbor of Road Town, Tortola.

CHAPTER V

TORTOLA

Road Harbour (H.O. Chart 0137) is six miles east of West End, Tortola. It was for many years the only port of entry in the British Virgins, but recently yachts have been permitted to enter at Soper's Hole. We had committed a breach of etiquette having landed at Norman before clearing at Road Town.

Entering we left the white conical buoy, marking Scotch Bank, to starboard, and proceeded directly for Government House, the only large white bastioned building between the western inner entrance and the town. Government House is also noteworthy for being set in a lush garden of fine trees with a very prominent cement water catchment area up the hillside above it.

On Burt Point, the western inner entrance, there stood for many years the ruins of Fort Burt. More recently an isolation hospital stood there. Later a very nice hotel was opened on Burt Point. The buildings were pink, and a Union Jack flew each day over them. Below the hotel, on the water's edge were two hangar-like buildings with bright blue doors. This was a boatyard. There were two range markers above the boatyard, a white diamond over a white triangle. We lined up on these and went in to about two hundred yards from the boatyard dock to anchor in two fathoms. Here we hung, headed southeast and protected by a reef and mangrove growth which flanked the entrance to a creek and careenage off the hotel. There is good holding

This Tortola trading schooner, becalmed in St. Thomas harbor, has come from the outer islands with a load of salt and charcoal.

ground here of sand and mud though a constant and gentle roll. Inside the creek was a good hurricane hole for small boats drawing up to five feet.

Soon after our hook went down our quarantine flag was answered by Customs official Jacobs who outboarded to us in a rowboat flying the Red Ensign. After taking the list of the ship's company and seeing our passports Officer Jacobs had a cup of coffee and gave us some of the latest news from ashore.

The regular Administrator, Jeffry Allsebrook, was presently at home on vacation leave to England. The acting Administrator, His Honour Edward A. Evelyn, had previously filled the post of Administrator so was called out of retirement by the British Government to sit in while Mr. Allsebrook was away. A very nice little cruising sloop, the *Arawak* which was anchored near us, belonged to the Acting Administrator. His Honour and Mrs. Evelyn had been ardent sailors, cruising *Arawak* up and down the islands in all kinds of weather. But, sadly, Mrs. Evelyn had died six months previous to our visit and the loss was a great shock to her husband. *Arawak* had been sitting idle for some time.

Mr. Jacobs told us that there were several developments ashore of local interest. A full time electric plant was now going and Tortola had a motion picture theater at last. Also for the first time a regular newspaper was about to make its debut, and a bank was about to be opened. These innovations marked the first signs of a commercial comeback since the devastating hurricane of 1924 laid the waterfront low.

We went ashore for cocktails and dinner at Fort Burt Hotel which was operated by a very gay and friendly couple, the Hammersleys. Over the ruins of the old fort they had put up several bungalows, a dining room, a cocktail lounge and a very tastefully furnished main lounge. Chris Hammersley was an Englishman, an ardent sailing enthusiast, and his wife Millie was an American with a great zest for living and gift of conversation. She had done so many things to improve conditions locally that a couple of years earlier she was on the Queen's Honours List and received the coveted M.B.E.

The Hammersley dining room was run as though the visiting customers were guests. Chris sat at the head of the table, Millie at the opposite end under a large portrait of herself in evening gown. The food was excellent,

When a boat comes into Road Town Harbor, with a load of fish, dockside shoppers soon buy it all. These are jacks which were sold at twenty cents a pound.

and fastidiously served and the conversation ranged from theater to music to horse racing to local anecdotes.

Millie had done a lot for morale when she began importing horses from St. Croix and entered her colors into the competition of the local track at Sea Cow Bay. Her horse *Three Aces* was called *"Tree Ace"* by the natives and they went wild every time the horse performed. He always came in first in the field of twenty to thirty horses that ran. The natives attributed this to some sort of magic on Millie's part for she always whispered in *Tree Ace's* ear just before a start. She also forbade her jockeys to ever whip or kick *Tree Ace* and said "just ride him—let the horse win on his own without urging." This had a good effect in offsetting the tendency among the natives to whip race their animals.

Noel Coward had been a guest of the Hammersleys the previous year. He came to Fort Burt to get away from his estate in Jamaica during the tourist season when curious visitors and friends gave him no peace.

After dinner Millie sat down at the grand piano in the sitting room and played for us. It was pleasant and intimate and once again we were amazed to see all the fragile furnishings one doesn't expect in a hotel in the tropics. The room was not large yet did not seem overcrowded with the crystals, porcelains and highly polished antique cabinets and breakfronts. On one wall was an especially fine portrait of Chris which had once hung in the Royal Academy. We had always heard that one must be very careful not to bring fragile things to islands in the Caribbean. Fungus, mildew, termites and bugs of every kind were supposed to ruin anything not of metal or concrete. But the truth is that only on islands where it rains heavily does real destruction take place. Of course, there are apt to be termites on any island but one can watch for them and check the woodwork from time to time. They only attack certain woods, never mahogany or any of the hard woods. When someone says he sat on a chair in the tropics and it disintegrated (I have read this in several books) you may be sure that the piece of furniture in question was (1) made of soft wood and (2) thoroughly neglected.

I have seen libraries on some of the wetter islands so riddled with worm holes and discolored by mildew I wondered before we came to live in the tropics if I should bring any very valuable volumes along. I brought all my best things. In ten years not a worm has appeared in any of my books. And none has suffered from mildew as they did each summer in our house in Connecticut. If one lives where the trade winds blow and windows and doors are open, as they are most of the time, the natural air-conditioning is amazingly kind to delicate possessions.

The Hammersleys kept two trim Tortola sloops in the careenage basin below the hotel and sailing-minded guests could use them to box around the harbor or take them for a picnic around to Sea Cow Bay. As before mentioned, Chris Hammersley was a keen sailor and with little urging liked to sail with his guests and point out the sights.

The next morning was Saturday and we went in to the town dock early to have a look at the weekly market. At the dock were sloops from East End and West End carrying vegetables and fish. The market is small, a few open stalls under some sheds at the head of the dock. Tortola Island is so steep-to all around that market goods come in either by boat or by muleback down the mountain sides. There is a road along the shore a few miles each side of town but only donkey trails above or beyond it. One scene of wild buying was centered around a sloop full almost to the gunwales with Jack-fish that had been netted that morning. One fisherman stood up to his knees in fish tossing handfuls into baskets which were swung to him and then weighed by his partner who manipulated a rusty hand scales.

Then, just as the Jack-fish sale was going into high gear, a bunch of baseball players in fancy new uniforms swarmed onto the dock. On the red jacket of each was the large lettering "Titley Tigers." We were told that the team, sponsored by Maurice Titley of Titley's General Store, Road Town, was about to embark by launch to play an exhibition game at Cruz Bay against a team sponsored by St. John's merchants, Mooie and Sewer.

In the market stalls we found plenty of fresh meat, but the cuts were without rhyme or reason. Whoever shouted the loudest got what he wanted. Everything was the same price, 50 cents per pound, and we were lucky to get enough meat for several meals—steaks which turned out to be as tender and delicious as Trader Vic's best.

TORTOLA

Ice at Road Town was 5 cents per pound. We took on enough to keep the meat from spoiling for a few days as well as greatly improving our drinks at cocktail time.

There were only a few whites on Tortola and about eight thousand negroes. Many of the locals were devout Christians and to minister to the spiritual needs of the Methodists was the Rev. Mullings whose church was just beyond the jail. We stopped by the jail on the way to visit the Rev. Mullings and talked to a pleasant man in blue denim who was sweeping the courtyard of the police station. There was only one prisoner on the books at the time, said the man in blue denim, "An' I am de prisonah." He was in for "borrowing" a neighbor's bicycle and with good behavior expected to be out by Christmas.

The Rev. Mullings and his family lived in a pleasant little wooden verandahed house above his church. He was a good-looking East Indian and most of his flock were farmers or cattle raisers in the mountains. Therefore the Rev. Mullings had no need for a car. He traveled about fifty miles a month by horseback.

Walking back through the dilapidated little town we passed many donkeys led down from the hills loaded with produce for market day. Many were in pairs, with the farmer or his wife riding one and leading the other. Near the market we met father J. N. Keith Gibson, head of the Anglican Church for the British Virgins. Father Gibson, in long white robe, sash and sandals reminded us of the French padres so prevalent in Martinique. But there are no Roman Catholic churches in these islands. We had tea on the verandah of Father Gibson's little cottage above his church and overlooking Road Town Harbour. Most of his parishioners lived along the eight miles of road between the village and Kingston Point and he made all his calls by motor scooter.

The lovely view from Father Gibson's porch appeared soon to be doomed. Rising between his rectory and the sea was an ambitious-looking hotel building, its gaunt outer walls of poured concrete jutting two stories up in the air. But the threatened black-out was not too imminent we learned. A New York syndicate had been fooling with putting up the building for the past four years and had apparently run out of funds. The structure in its present condition was merely an eyesore through which one could still see the view.

[65]

We had made these calls along the narrow shore road east of town. In the other direction we passed a series of little shops containing groceries and hardware and sundries. The prices were about the same as St. Thomas which is not at all bad, considering that everything is shipped in from St. Thomas or England. A few yards beyond the congested part of the town we came upon a two-story blue cement structure with a great deal of remodeling-bustle going on. While we stood aside as a truck full of cement backed in and blocked the unfinished façade at the entrance, a voice called down from a balcony overhead.

"Hello Eunice. I just spotted *Renegade* and was about to come out and say hello. Come in and let me show you how the wheels of progress are turning."

"Well, Norman, what on earth are you doing here? Last I heard of you you were on Anegada raising sharks."

"Not raising them, my dear, catching them. I was shipping shark hides to New Jersey. I'll tell you all about that, but first come up and see the new cinema."

We were introduced to a slim, earnest and ascetic-looking Englishman in his early thirties who was as far from the stereotyped movie version of the rum-soaked loafer in the tropics as one could imagine.

Earlier Norman Fowler and Edward Allcard had sailed the twelve ton *Catania* across the Atlantic from England to the West Indies. This was the Edward Allcard who had previously twice crossed the Atlantic single-handed. He had joined Fowler on the *Catania* in order to collect a boat in which he (Allcard) was going on some further voyaging. In St. Thomas Fowler had sold the *Catania* and decided to settle in the Virgin Islands.

Norman's first venture, the shark project on remote Anegada, had ended in failure. He had sunk $16,000 in his belief that a fishermen's cooperative could be established which would raise the standard of living of the poor people of the outer islands. But it turned out that the fishermen had been so long accustomed to an every-man-for-himself existence that they just wouldn't cooperate either with Fowler or each other. The more of his money he poured in to make the venture go, the more suspicious the natives became of the whole idea. He had then come to Tortola deciding that to "do good" one must not necessarily give things away.

His latest was a three-pronged venture all beginning with the letter T like Titley's Tigers. On the ground floor, rear, of his new building he was installing the presses for his new newspaper, *The Tortola Times*. On the ground floor, front, he was installing a large vault just shipped from England to grace the offices of his newly formed bank, *The Tortola Trust Co.* Upstairs he had installed a movie projector, a sound system and some hundred seats for his cinema, *The Tortola Theater*. Counting standing room he could take in one hundred fifty people each performance. He had been showing pictures even though the building was unfinished and had capacity houses at each of the four performances per week. His movie was already grossing him $1,200 per month.

Whenever Norman goes to England he looks for old books about the West Indies and especially for anything about Tortola. He showed us a first edition account of a celebrated slave case which was published in London in 1812:

A REPORT OF THE TRIAL
OF ARTHUR HODGE, ESQ.
(Late one of the members of His
Majesty's Council for the
Virgin Islands)
AT THE ISLAND OF TORTOLA
ON THE 25th APRIL, 1811
FOR THE MURDER OF HIS
NEGRO MAN SLAVE NAMED PROSPER

Hodge thought of himself as a pious man but he was in fact a sadist and punished his slaves for any little infraction of his rules. The white community must have had enough of Hodge, for when word got around that his man Prosper died after a flogging, the Public Treasury appropriated £600 and brought a special Crown prosecutor out from England to see that Hodge met the fate he deserved. It is noted in the book that Hodge spent £900 on his defense. Crown attorneys tore Hodge's defense to ribbons and the final summation to the jury is a masterpiece of rhetoric.

The defendant was found guilty and sentenced to death by hanging in the public square. On the scaffold Hodge gave a little speech saying he was sorry for what he had done; then turned to the Methodist minister who attended him and bowed his head in prayer. The book ends: "At the awful signal he was launched into eternity."

Even though the Hodge case took place on one of the most insignificant spots in the British Empire it was quoted round the world and was used by the growing forces for emancipation to hasten the day of abolition.

At the time of Hodge's launching into eternity, sugar was king in the Caribbean and Tortola was at the very peak of prosperity. There were then one hundred thirty sugar estates on the island, owned by one thousand whites and worked by seven thousand slaves. It is hard to imagine that the steep hillsides, where today hardly a goat can get a foothold, were once planted almost to their summits with cane.

The hanging of Hodge didn't bring Prosper back to life. It is even probable that the deliberately slow steady grinding of the wheels of justice, British fashion, was misunderstood by the seething army of blacks working from dawn to dusk. Prosper's life or any of theirs might be taken by a white man's whim in a matter of minutes. These same masters took weeks of speech-making to bring retribution to one of their own.

At any rate it is recorded that the seething continued and in 1831 a slave plot was discovered—a plot to murder all whites on Tortola and commandeer ships for escape to Haiti. Word was gotten to St. Thomas just in time and the Danes sent a man-o-war, the St. Jan, to Road Harbour. This affair so frightened the whites that many of the planters and their families left the island. Those who remained mistakenly decided that more ruthlessness rather than less was the only way to insure their safety.

When news of official emancipation came out from London in 1834 the hard-core whites took the money Parliament awarded them in payment for their freed slaves but made wages so low and taxes so high that the negroes were in many cases worse off than before. The final straw came when a white man killed a negro during an argument over the taxing of a cow.

By pre-arrangement one of the ex-slaves blew a blast on the conch shell. Echoing blasts were repeated 'round the island. In twenty-four hours all the great houses were torn down, their contents plundered and burned and all whites were massacred with the exception of four who got away in a rowboat and made it through The Narrows to St. John. Ironically enough King Cane, the despot who had in his name virtually created slavery in the Caribbean, had abdicated and now no one cared what happened on Tortola. The world market for sugar had fallen as beet-root sugar had begun to be manufactured in Europe and the sugar islands were suddenly worthless.

The cane fields of Tortola reverted to the men who had created them, and by the time British officials were once again in residence on Tortola everything, including the ruins of the great houses, had gone back to bush.

In the high country there is a kind of outside-the-law independence practiced by the natives to this day. No money changes hands up there we were told. A brand of white rum which they manufacture and pass around in demijohns is the only currency. This is used to pay people who work the few cane fields that exist to produce rum, and to barter for cattle which is the main source of outside revenue for the hill-toppers. The mountain people resent any census-taking, either of themselves or their cattle and keep alive their ancient resistance to taxation in any form.

Opposite the dock is the post office and above it is the office of the Administrator. I dropped in to leave my card and try to arrange an appointment and was surprised when His Honour's pretty colored secretary disappeared for a few minutes and returned to say: "Come right in; Mr. Evelyn will see you now."

I was uneasy when I suddenly found myself shaking hands with a good-looking middle-aged Britisher in a white starched suit and an old school tie.

"I just asked for an appointment. I didn't expect to call in my wrinkled sailing shorts and old sneakers," I said.

"Just the thing. I wish I were dressed as you are myself. Sit down

Tortola marine architect Noel Duff Richardson designer and contractor of the *Christmas Eve* stands on the right proudly pointing out a feature of the framing of his unfinished craft.

and tell me how the cruising's going. I've seen *Renegade* in here before. A nice ship."

Renegade and Mr. Evelyn's *Arawak* looked jaunty sitting in the blue harbor framed by his window. I told him I had rowed around *Arawak* and admired her lines. When I asked who designed her he said he had himself. He had her built in St. Kitts. He and his wife had had some wonderful cruising in her. But things were different now. He had some inquiries to sell *Arawak* and perhaps he would. He was thinking of going to Canada where his two sons were in school. Would he miss the sailing paradise that is here? This couldn't be the same for him without his wife, he said.

When I shook hands in leaving he said: "Why don't you and your wife come to Government House for a drink around six-thirty this evening. You can land at the small pier where I keep my dinghy." This spontaneous hospitality is very typical of English officials we have met in the Caribbean Islands.

I picked up Hazel in the post office and told her we had a cocktail date at G.H. at 6:30 and the little preoccupied frown which I knew so well crossed her face.

"What are you pondering, dear?" I asked.

"Whether or not to risk wearing my pretty pink dress in the dinghy," was her prompt reply.

We walked back along the shore road to Fort Burt Hotel and paid a call at the Tortola Boat Yard. The Yard railway could haul boats up to six-foot draft and the proprietors had no plans for anything bigger. The equipment was good and we were told that a new steel cradle was presently on its way out from England.

Behind the boatyard a large craft was abuilding. Two native men had been working on the project for over a year and had gotten as far as keel and ribs. We talked to Noel McDuff Richardson, the designer, contractor and master carpenter of the 85 foot vessel-to-be and he introduced us to his seventy-year-old helper Lawrence Hope. The Messrs. Richardson and Hope were proud of the ship they had been toiling on for so long and we climbed all over it admiring the great gnarled natural knees and outsized frames. The previous Christmas Eve they had contracted to build the ship for a Tortola cattle man who didn't know too much about the sea.

"It will be schooner-rigged of course," I observed.

"It should be, but de owner he say he like one big mast so it have to be a sloop."

"What will you call her?"

"De owner he call her *Christmas Eve* in honor of de occasion when he gib me de contract."

The *Christmas Eve* understandably had no firm launching date. It looked from where we stood as though Noel McDuff Richardson and his helper had several years work ahead of them. Delivered complete with a diesel engine the vessel was to stand the owner $32,000.

"De owner he plan to gib a big party on de day ob de launching," said aged Helper Hope optimistically as we parted.

It was late afternoon when we hailed *Renegade,* and Eunice and Felix dinghied in to the dock. Eunice was on her way up to the Hammersleys' for cocktails and we told her that after we returned from Government House we would come in and join her.

Hazel and I showered aboard *Renegade* and dressed in our best for our cocktail date. Mr. Evelyn met us at the entrance to Government House, we signed the guest book and he showed us upstairs to a large sitting room opening on a verandah with another of those breath-taking Virgin Island views. An afterglow of sunset vermilion beyond a cluster of pink-tinted clouds emphasized the silhouetted islands across Sir Francis Drake Channel. Soon a few town lights were twinkling and we could see *Renegade*'s riding light, a tiny pin-point far out.

A very good springboard for conversation when talking to any sailing-minded Englishman is to mention Uffa Fox, Britain's most colorful designer and builder of small racing craft.

I had met Uffa and gone for a dinghy sail with him back in 1936 when he came to the U. S. with T. O. M. Sopwith to race on *Endeavour*. Uffa was then at the threshold of his career. He had sailed an Uffa Fox-designed dinghy across the English Channel and in 1936 brought a racing dinghy over to challenge the American Canoe Association for the large assortment of trophies which had up to then never left U. S. shores. He raced the cream of America's sailing canoe experts and took all the trophies back to England where they have ever since remained.

Mr. Evelyn smiled at my enthusiastic gambits about Uffa and quickly turned the conversation to more recent history.

"Let's talk about the latest *America's* Cup fiasco. It seems to me your chaps made the competition look rather like a Brixham Trawler."

Hazel and I had followed the *America's* Cup Races with a group of English friends on St. Lucia and each day as the "wireless" had spelled out the details we had found it more and more difficult to think up words of comment. The rout finally had been so complete that the most ardent British fan had to say to us: "Don't try to say 'Good Show' or anything like that. We put up a rotten show, in fact wasted a blasted lot of good money and time on no show at all. We should chuck it and let the Canadians or the Australians challenge next time—if there is a next time."

To Mr. Evelyn, Hazel said: "A lot of our American Sailing friends were not cheering for our side. It would be a good thing for yachting if the *America's* Cup would change hands for a few seasons."

"I doubt if we could keep it five minutes. Look how your fellows have been turning up regularly to wallop us in the Fastnet. The Fastnet is the one race we should know most about. Apparently you could come over and beat us in a knitting basket."

When we parted Mr. Evelyn asked us to come by any afternoon; the house, he said, was a rather lonesome place and he liked company. We said we planned to sail early next morning and were very grateful for his hospitality.

We had quite a ride from Government House dock to *Renegade*. The wind had piped up from southeast and dumped a rain squall on us half way out. Between the rain, and the chop spraying over the dinghy, we were thoroughly drenched in the only Sunday clothes we had brought along on the cruise. Eunice was already aboard. She had been ferried out by a Hammersley dinghy just before the squall broke.

Rufus had borrowed a charcoal brazier from somewhere and treated us to broiled Tortola steak, cole slaw and hot local rolls and garlic butter. By 8:30 we were all in our bunks.

The mangrove growth on the dry reef which shielded us to windward afforded perfect protection but even so, a gentle swell came through to make a slight but steady pitch all night. Sometimes it is easier to fall asleep when a boat is pitching heavily than when the pitch is gentle. With a heavy pitch there is such a jumble of noises as things on deck and below rattle around that it becomes a symphony with no one noise outstanding. The gentle pitch of our Road Harbour anchorage brought several regular sounds which were most tantalizing to try to identify. I found myself counting the cadence of a cockpit block clicking softly with the monotonous regularity of a slow metronome. Then I decided this sound must be something slightly ajar in the galley. When I got up to investigate I found that the sliding door to the head was tapping softly with each pitch. I put a cardboard wedge in it and went back to my bunk and listened. The block-clicking had now ceased aft and a double clicking of two blocks ticked off the time from up forward.

Then there was the bouncing ball sound. Right after each pitch there were three taps from somewhere near the base of the mainmast. These sounded just like the tired last bounces of a ping pong ball. I whispered across to Hazel; she had been counting the bouncing ball too and was quite awake. She thought it sounded as though a child's marble was loose on the book shelf of the dog house and rolled in such a way as to make three bounces every ten seconds. Again I got up to investigate and this time found Eunice exploring the dog house with a flashlight.

"That bouncing ball sound is a new one," said Eunice. "I can't figure out what it is."

The three of us went up on deck and listened. Now there were so many noises there was not a chance to single out the subtle one that had been keeping us awake. Everything was slightly arustle with the wind. *Skipperkey* thought we were about to be boarded and stood over the swimming ladder and barked. We heard an answering bark from shore and then a loud whinny from *Tree Ace* on the hillside above Fort Burt. All the squall clouds had cleared away and every star in the heavens was out. We sat enthralled in the cockpit and picked out some of the familiar constellations. Orion's Belt was almost directly overhead. The buckle looked close enough to touch the top of our mainmast which seemed to be pointing it out with each pitch of *Renegade*. Off to the south a falling star made a fiery mark across the sky as it burned itself out over Peter Island.

We resolved (as we always did when under a tropic sky on a clear night) to pay more attention to the sheer beauty of the universe. We thought with pity of the thousands of highly-trained men of science who at that very moment were stationed around the world meticulously plotting the skies for future wars.

We were off at dawn and with the wind still south of east we were able to make The Bluff at the southern tip of Beef Island on a long tack. As we passed Nora Hazel (no kin) Point on Tortola we were close enough to study quite a mansion erected there by an American, high above the sea. It is a Greek Temple with four pillars surmounted by a pediment of classic proportions. Since there are no other houses in sight for miles in either direction there is nothing to clash with it. If someone came along and put a California ranch house on one side of it and someone else put a tile-roofed Italian villa on the other, Nora Hazel Point might begin to look like a Caribbean version of Disneyland.

As we passed The Bluff and saw Virgin Gorda's Mountain Point far to the northeast we noticed something bright red bobbing about in the middle distance.

"Looks like a red buoy up there," Hazel said.

"Can't be unless it is something that has gone adrift from Spain."

The 6:55 weather broadcast from Puerto Rico had been warning mariners to look out for a drifting buoy somewhere to westward. No buoy could drift eastward hereabouts.

I put the binoculars on the tiny triangle of red and saw that it was moving. Soon it rose high enough above a trough so I could see that it was a tiny sailboat.

CHAPTER VI

BEEF ISLAND

WE JIBED over as we came around the eastern shore of Beef and headed for the almost landlocked Trellis Bay, Beef Island. Drawing Trellis Bay abeam one sees a tiny cay sitting in the middle of the entrance. This is called Bellamy Cay and has a low hotel-building of field stone on it. There are two rocks to be avoided just outside the eastern passage into Trellis Bay. Yachts of any size should enter the western passage leaving the hotel to port and lining up with the center of the passage.

Trellis Bay at the time of our visit was a very bustling yacht spot. It had the only marine railway between Martinique and Puerto Rico capable of hauling vessels drawing over six feet. The yard and hotel were at the time being operated by two young Americans, Ed Karkow and Dick Newick, and they were doing such an efficent job that vessels were coming to them from all over the area. They had a perpetual waiting list and as Hazel remarked: "They are so busy it is like getting an appointment with the only hairdresser in a small town." We had been relaying messages on our radio all along on the cruise from yachts trying to get appointments to be hauled at Beef.

There were six yachts at anchor when we sailed in. (By the way, everyone *sails* into Trellis. To power in would be to lose face in this salty company.) A 78 foot schooner from Puerto Rico was the largest. The 30 foot yawl *Stout* which Ed Karkow had sailed over from Den-

A native trading schooner and a yacht are hauled together on the Trellis Bay
slipway at Beef. Behind them is Great Camanoe. To the right are Scrub Island
and Marina Cay.

Eunice, Hazel and *Skipperkey* take a stroll on the beach at Beef Island. Beyond *Renegade,* upper left, is the Trellis Bay "club" on Bellamy Cay. At right are *Ay-Ay* and *Stout.*

mark was the smallest. An unusual sight in such a remote spot was a 40 foot catamaran, the *Ay Ay*, built and owned by Dick Newick. There was also a 50 ton native schooner from Tortola and a Brixham Trawler which had been converted into a yacht and sailed from Portsmouth, England.

The western tip enclosing the bay is called Buccaneer Point and on it is a pretty bungalow of field stone which was built by the former manager-owner of the place, another round-the-world yachtsman, Wladyslau Wagner. The Wagners were off for several months' visit in the States and had leased the operation to Ed Karkow for a couple of years. Just beyond the Wagner house and facing east was the marine railway. Beyond the railway a tree-shaded swimming beach extended across the head of the bay. On this beach Ed and Dick were putting the finishing touches on four small attractive housekeeping cottages which would be for rental in the winter season. They also planned to set up a small food-shopping center on the hotel isle.

After anchoring we took the dinghy over to the Cay and were welcomed by Dick and Ed, both old friends of Eunice's. The bar, lounge and terrace of the "Trellis Bay Club" were attractive and faced a lovely vista of rolling hills and high peaks with the translucent blue of the anchorage in the foreground.

As we were being shown around we walked along the sea-wall facing north and again voiced the familiar cliché, "Gosh, there are islands everywhere."

Great Camanoe, Scrub, Little Camanoe and Guana rose around us giving Trellis Bay protection from every angle northward.

"That's Marina Cay over there, sitting on the passage between Scrub and Great Camanoe," said Dick. "You can just see a bit of the house on top. The house Robb White and his wife Rodie built."

We had read OUR VIRGIN ISLAND, the book Robb White had written, describing the trials and tribulations they had gone through building and living on Marina Cay. Now, as we watched, the little boat with the red sails came opposite and hailed us.

"Quite a jaunty sight to see a little sloop with red sails in this far-away place," I remarked. "We spotted them far up Drake Channel as we headed in."

"That's the Helsleys. Charley and his wife and baby have been living up on Anegada. He's a geologist. Collects rocks. We'll have a drink with them later."

"Pretty fancy, those red sails."

Ed laughed. "Charley couldn't help the red sails. A movie company has been out here filming OUR VIRGIN ISLAND and they had to have color in every shot. They paid Charley well for renting his boat but they ruined the sails. They had no red dye so painted the sails red with housepaint."

"Must have been a lot of excitement on Marina Cay," I ventured.

"No. They took one look at Marina Cay and went off and built themselves a more photogenic setting."

The movie people had visualized a lush tropical isle circled with a beach of talcum-powder sand under a fringe of coconut palms. Marina Cay looks just like Scrub Island which rises behind it. No beaches, no border of swaying palms. Just a few low trees and scrubby bush. The Cay was mostly bare and rocky with cactus growing here and there. You can walk completely round the rocky shore in half an hour.

Certainly one can use almost every praising adjective in the dictionary when describing the Virgin Islands. But one thing they are not. In the traditional sense of what a lush tropical island is supposed to be, they are quite dissimilar to the island paradises of song and story.

Perhaps the trouble all started with Herman Melville. When he returned from the South Seas to write TYPEE and OMOO the idea of tropical island paradises first became implanted in the mind of civilized man. It meant islands of dense jungle growth, waterfalls, exotic flowers. It meant miles and miles of white sand beaches shaded by thousands of coconut palms. Of course it meant romance too, with beautiful native maidens who bathed under the waterfalls as singing birds in brilliant plumage darted in and out of the great trees.

It meant the Tahiti of Pierre Loti and Paul Gauguin. All this idea of jungles, waterfalls, flowers, beaches and palms was no myth to be exploded by later writers. Nordhoff and Hall found it too. Hazel and I found it when we spent months sailing around the Polynesian Islands between Tahiti and Raratonga.

We are often asked what we think of the Virgin Islands as compared

[80]

with the Tahitian Islands. Both areas are sailing paradises for the yachtsman. But in a word, the difference is rainfall. Tahiti has mile-high peaks to catch the clouds and fill its lakes, rivers and streams and nourish its forests. As all the Virgin Islands are relatively low, rainfall is often a problem. A governor of Danish times is quoted in Westergaard's THE DANISH WEST INDIES as writing, "We have had no rain for 6 months and the cane is drying up in the fields." A cattle man on Tortola says he lives in mortal fear of drought. He told us he never knows when a dry period will strike and he will have to cope with it by shipping off all his animals for slaughter.

Charles Helsley and his beautiful blonde wife soon joined us on the terrace. They seemed to consider sailing around the islands in an 18 foot sloop as merely routine. They had sailed the dozen miles from Gorda Sound and across Drake Channel to Beef in two and a half hours and their three months' old baby had slept peacefully all the way. It was lucky they were on a run before the wind for they had almost no freeboard. Besides considerable luggage the boat was loaded with specimens of rock Charles was bringing back to the States. We thought how much handier it would be to collect butterflies. The Helsleys had been on Anegada several weeks while he was completing the research necessary to win his Master's degree when he returned to his studies at Princeton.

We had never experienced sailing in a catamaran and next morning when Dick invited us for a Sunday sail we were delighted. The Helsleys had sailed off early for St. Thomas. The yacht *Jacinta* had had a haulout at Beef and her owners, Mr. and Mrs. Johnson, generously took them, their baby and the pile of assorted rocks along.

The *Ay Ay* (ancient Carib name for St. Croix) had been built on St. Croix by Dick. Before he met Ed and went into the boat yard business he had used it to take charter parties from Christiansted to Buck Island for picnicking. The bridge deck of a 40 foot catamaran is enormous. It can easily accommodate twenty passengers on the two long seats that face each other and stretch from hull to hull.

With Dick's attractive wife, Pat, manning the twin rudders, the *Ay Ay* went shooting out the channel between the Camanoes like a streak. We had a little trouble coming about a couple of times. The boat tends to come half way around and hang in irons. Dick has been experimenting with leeboards to give the hulls more bite in the water. At first the air was spotty and light, with so many islands rising all around us, but we picked up a fair breeze as we got farther out. There is a sensation of flying when a well-balanced cat' moves in a fair breeze. For a half hour we flew along at ten to twelve knots. Dick has done over twenty knots in *Ay Ay* on several occasions. He and Pat had sailed it the forty miles back and forth from St. Croix to St. Thomas a dozen times in all kinds of weather. The twin hulls have over six foot headroom with bunks and living accommodations below for four people. But the hulls are too narrow and cramped to be considered comfortable quarters at sea. Dick admits that his cat' should in no way be confused with a cruising boat. But he wouldn't hesitate to take it down the eight hundred mile chain of islands to Trinidad. The yacht could make such fast passages between the islands as to be sure of anchorages each night.

As we were sailing back toward Trellis, I joined Dick on the after deck where he was lying on his back maneuvering the long helm connecting the two rudders. His face had the expression of pure contentment.

Dick had been an ardent sailor as long as he could remember. Three years before he had sailed through many of the canals of Europe, then had joined the 40 foot cutter *Adara* at Gibraltar and sailed out to the Caribbean. He had fallen in love with the islands and with Pat, had married in St. Croix and hopes to spend the rest of his life in the Virgins building and sailing boats.

"Dick," I said, pointing to the islands that circled us; "If you were describing these islands to someone who had never seen them how would you do it?"

"I'd say they reminded me most of the foothills around San Francisco Bay. There is a part of St. Thomas that looks just like the Marin County hills. That part of Tortola there could be one of the Berkeley Hills above the University campus."

Dick had found the description I had long had in the back of my mind. I hadn't known until then that Dick, too, had gone to the University of California. His class was much more recent than mine but we both knew the area well enough to make comparisons. Dick also added

On one of our visits to Tortola we met these three baseball stars and their coach as they were about to debark with their team mates for a challenge game on St. John.

to our collection of stories about *Lystria*. She had been hauled out at Beef the year before and it was decided that some of her plates were so thin they couldn't risk chipping off rust!

After *Ay Ay* was once again secured on her mooring Hazel and I took a walk to the West End of Beef Island. Here Beef comes so close to Tortola that there was a little do-it-yourself ferry to carry the boat-yard workers to and fro. We have been in many warm places in our travels but the two-mile walk to the ferry and back was as hot as any we ever experienced. Part of the distance had been bulldozed to put in an airstrip to give Tortola air contact with the world. It is hard to realize that of Tortola's total area, comprising some twenty-one square miles, there was no practical place to put an airstrip. For a piece of land twelve miles long this is something of a record.

Being Sunday the bulldozers were quiet and the dust not as bad as it might have been. Just before we reached the ferry we passed the ruins of a former Great House. The vines and bush had so closed the old walls in that we found it impossible to go to it, although it was only a few feet off the road. The ferry was quite an arrangement. A pontoon-like barge, capable of carrying a dozen people, was tethered to a steel cable in such a way that by pulling a rope secured to either shore transportation could be accomplished. A snag came when someone absentmindedly secured the barge to one shore. Then the person on the other shore who wanted it had to swim across.

There was a dense mangrove growth bordering the shallows near the ferry. Here we saw a pair of white heron fishing. Birds are of especial interest in these islands because aside from sea birds few are seen. There are still some of the pretty little ground doves—the turtle dove from which Tortola got its name. We saw three pair of these being stalked by a mongoose on the road ahead of us as we walked back to Trellis Bay. I later asked about the scarcity of bird life on Tortola and was told that hurricane and drought were equally responsible for driving the birds away from the islands. We could also believe the claim that the mongoose, which was originally imported to rid the cane of rats, had long since grown tired of rat meat and turned to birds.

Scattered all over Beef Island are large boulders of a variety of granite. This is what has supplied the building stone for the Trellis Bay

Hotel as well as the old Great Houses. Our friends Ed and Dick said they visited the remains of a remarkable Great House which was half way up the slope of the high hill east of the anchorage.

Robb White described the remains of a Great House (probably the same one) which he and his wife found under the bush on the hill behind Trellis Bay anchorage. He found blocks and columns of marble, the remains of a slate roof, and some remnants of wall standing around a ballroom that had been one hundred feet long. He saw no signs of fire and none of earthquake and concluded that the building had been destroyed by human hands at the time of the rebellion of the ex-slaves. The Whites (this was in the late '30s) found an old lady, a Mrs. Brodie, who had lived on Beef Island some forty years and professed to know something of the history of the place. She said the Great House had been occupied in 1724 by a widow named Catherine George. The Widow George raised fine cattle in the Beef Island tradition, and resented the raids that pirates made on her livestock. White says that once upon a time when a band of pirates had assembled to careen their ships at Marina Cay the Widow George invited them all over for a party. All came—some thirty-six buccaneers—and soon after festivities began thirty-six were carried out of the house on planks and buried on the beach with their bellies full of poisoned tea. We decided Robb White erred and really meant poisoned rum.

Robb White's wife Rodie once took a horseback ride up in the hills behind Road Town and saw the remains of an even greater Great House. Robb found the ruins of one on Great Camanoe and checked the records to discover this one had belonged to one Mary Vanterpool, a widow who in 1754 married "James Parke, a widower of Guanah Island."

Up and down the islands from Haiti to South America the ruins of these once proud palaces of the sugar barons lie in tumbled confusion under bush and jungle creepers. The 18th century phrase "rich as a West Indian planter" can be readily understood as one pokes around among the rubble—remains of patios and verandahs of Italian marble and bits of fluted columns imported from the islands of Greece.

Thomas Lynch who was one of the early sugar barons of Jamaica, was also Governor of that island. The fortune he amassed was so great that he was able to loan King Charles II £50,000. Shortly after the loan was arranged Lynch was knighted and henceforward known as Sir Thomas. Governor Lynch was a frequent visitor at Court and created quite a sensation as he was driven about the streets of London in his great gilded coach drawn by elaborately caparisoned horses shod with silver.

Renegade had not been hauled for six months and on Monday morning there was a slight hitch in the other appointments and the railway was suddenly free. We hailed Dick and Ed and by 10 A.M. were high and dry.

I rode around in the boat yard punt as Dick supervised the hauling. In a U. S. yard the great cradle goes down almost exactly arranged to take the waiting hull. On Trellis with so much diving man-power available and with the crystal-clear water, just the carriage of the cradle is rolled down the tracks under the hull. Then the divers get busy, four or five of them swimming in circles to call up the exact positioning as hull settles onto cradle and props are bolted in position.

Some workmen are on shore with ropes from the bow, others maneuver kedge anchors off the stern. A small army of very talented black men handle the boat as easily as a platoon of ants carry a dead moth. In the U. S. where even unskilled yard hands get $30.00 a day, as few men as possible are used during the hauling of a boat. And this is why we saw a 40 foot cutter roll out of its cradle in Darien just before we left Connecticut.

I tried to get some pictures as the begoggled Beef Island divers were scrambling under water and bringing up reports. But I should have had a movie camera with sound to catch the action.

First Diver: "Two foot water under she now."
Dick: "Pull that bow rope Henry. Let the kedge go a little Hugh."
Second Diver: "De bow she off de cradle dat way."
Dick: "Henry, get Jack and Ozzie and pull harder. Go on now pull like hell."
Third Diver: "Han me de big sledge suh."
Dick: "Where's the bow?"

Renegade was on the ways at Beef Island just long enough to get two coats of anti-fouling and a new water line. Yachts once came from all over the Caribbean for service at this yard.

Fourth Diver: "She one foot to go suh."
    Dick: "Henry, Ozzie, Jack, pull, pull harder you guys."
First Diver: "De bow she on."
    Dick: "Shorings, wedges get 'em up there forward."

Ten minutes later *Renegade* stood dripping in the yard and Jack, Henry, Ozzie, Hugh and a dozen other hands were busy with brooms and buckets. Eunice brought her own paint. The bottom was wire-brushed down, two coats of anti-fouling were applied, topsides were touched up and a new water-line painted in. Next morning *Renegade* was back on her mooring and the total bill was $117.00.

I remembered some of our experiences with our 34 foot Alden cutter *Tiare* which we sailed several seasons on Long Island Sound. One fall I had to go to Europe on business and instructed the yard to haul the boat for the winter while we were away. When we returned we opened our mail to find a long itemized bill from the boat-yard. I still remember that bill and especially the final item of 75 cents. This is the way it went:

To towing boat to yard	$35.00
To building cradle	45.00
To winterizing motor	40.00
To taking out mast	32.50
To hauling	51.00
To cleaning bottom and one coat of primer	47.50
To installing winter cover	42.00
To Storage (½)	34.00
To battery removal and maintenance	12.00
To sandpaper	.75
	$339.75

I had opened the bill and said to Hazel: "This is awful, but we did have one or two good sails this season. And why don't you get yourself some new clothes, Honey?"

[88]

This is the full-grown southern ray which Felix and Rufus landed after a touch and go battle. The long tail carries a vicious looking barb that can inflict real punishment.

This is a typical half-hour's spear gunning catch, tossed on deck from the boarding ladder. The baby ray is just the right size to yield tender non-oily meat.

[89]

The bill certainly was awful, but I consoled myself thinking of the fun I would have going to the yard next evening after a hard day at the office and admiring the beautiful thing I had worked so many years to possess. Next evening Hazel met me at the 6:02 and we drove directly to the boat-yard. But we walked all over the yard and couldn't find the boat.

"This is peculiar," I said. "I wonder if another yard hauled *Tiare*." "But these are the people who sent the bill," said Hazel.

We walked out beyond the yard onto the wooden pier. The tide was out and the scene was lifeless except for a few gulls who were padding around in the blue gunk looking for clams. Sitting in the mud beside the dock, her once snow-white topsides awash with slime, was *Tiare*. They had removed her sticks but that was all that had been done. She was a mess from stem to stern.

Next morning I called the yard from my office in New York. They were sorry and guessed the bookkeeper had made a mistake. I could take *Tiare* to another yard if I chose to do so. (They knew as well as I that all the yards were full.)

There are some fine, unspoiled coral gardens around the rocks off the Wagner cottage at Trellis Bay. Rufus and Felix spent a lot of time in the water after hours and spear-gunned enough fish to greatly augment the food supply. But they found it hard to resist any swimming thing that came their way. They were especially skilled at diving to the bottom in fifteen or twenty feet of water and looking under ledges and toppling over loose coral that sometimes had a lobster under it. Eunice had told them to look for baby rays and not bother the larger ones. The rays swim along the bottom foraging for shell-fish and when they are through feeding are hard to see as they lie motionless with their tails and outer edges hidden under the sand.

One day Rufus spotted a fully grown southern ray and couldn't resist the shot. Felix and the dinghy were fifty feet off as the spear took hold and due to the short line it looked for a couple of minutes as though Rufus must either let go his gun or drown. But he held his breath and the ray luckily swam in the direction of the dinghy. Here Felix got another spear in him and both boys hung onto their guns with one hand and the dinghy with the other until the ray was exhausted

A swimmer has to be very fast to catch one of these hawkbill turtles under water. But the hawkbill is not an especially edible variety and we let our Beef Island catch go.

and boated. The dinghy was dragged round and round in circles for fifteen minutes before the struggle was over. The same afternoon Felix spotted a young turtle in the water off the point. He came upon him so unexpectedly the turtle didn't have a chance. The boys outdove him with such speed they were able to grab him from the rear. But he was a hawk-bill, not good eating even though half grown, so we made some pictures and set him free.

CHAPTER VII

GUANA ISLAND

WITH *Renegade's* hauling job completed we decided to sail around and visit Guana Island. Again we went through the narrow channel between the Camanoes. Then, when well through (taking care to give the reef east of the north tip of Little Camanoe plenty of room), we headed due west for Monkey Point, the southernmost piece of Guana. The day started off bright and clear but by the time we were attempting to anchor off the sand beach below the cluster of cottages on the hill in White Bay a series of rain squalls was greeting us. This is usually a quiet spot, well-protected for running ashore with a dinghy. Oddly enough after the first squall the wind whipped around from the west and we were soon dragging the big Danforth. We put on the diesel, the boys wound up the chain and we tried once again to anchor, this time a little farther out.

The rain ceased, the sun reappeared and the standard wind came to us from the east over the island. But when we powered in reverse to see how well we were holding we discovered that the anchor had not bitten at all. One hundred fifty feet of chain was out in four fathoms and we dragged as easily as though chain and anchor had parted company. Rufus swam down to the end of the chain and came back to report that the anchor was still there and not dug in. As Rufus pulled himself hand over hand up the chain and onto the bow a rain squall hit us so hard we decided it wasn't our day to visit Guana.

THE VIRGIN ISLANDS

There was no particular reason for going ashore. The owners of Guana, Louis and Beth Bigelow, were in the U. S. visiting and the place was closed up. The Bigelows are another pair of Americans who fell in love with the islands and bought one. They came to the Virgins in the 30's and set up Guana as a club where several of their stateside friends come each winter on holiday and share expenses. It is a fine reciprocal arrangement and has resulted in the Bigelows finding several houses open to them when they visit in the U. S. in the off season.

With the anchor on deck we discovered what had been the cause of the trouble. The tips of the two blades had been bent so that if the anchor lay scooping upward there was no chance of digging in. If it lay with the bend downward it would dig in more efficiently than an ordinary unsprung Danforth. This was a Mark IV, high tensile steel job and not supposed to bend too easily. But some weeks before, *Renegade* had spent two days at anchor off Anegada Island facing strong winds and with a very heavy swell. The Danforth was holding in coral rock and during moments of greatest strain, each time *Renegade* was brought up hard, the flukes were subjected to terrific pressure. It is no criticism of the Danforth to say that the flukes were slightly bent. The fact that it held and only developed a small bend is a tribute to Mr. Danforth. Many another anchor would have broken under such punishment.

We had been lucky that the anchor had landed on the biting side in all our anchorages thus far. It should, we thought, begin now to average out and fall on the wrong side for a time. We had Rufus check it from here on and surprisingly it landed wrong side down at every anchorage for the remainder of the cruise. So Rufus had to swim down to it and turn it over each time. Just as a tossed coin is supposed to land with an equal number of heads and tails after a million tosses, but will often run a long series of tails and a long series of heads (which makes gambling such a gamble), so apparently will an anchor behave. It defied every effort of ours to control it from above. No matter how carefully it was lowered it perversely flopped wrong side up. We would have to await our return to St. Thomas where some heavy machine shop equipment was available for straightening high tensile steel.

Guana Island is over eight hundred feet high and a mile and half

long. On the bluff separating White Bay and Muskmelon Bay a curious rock formation protrudes and is sculptured by nature to look exactly like the head of a lizard. The Iguana is a large lizard and from this
rock the island gets its name. Sometimes the name is corrupted to
Guano (bird droppings) which is incorrect. The PILOT lists a good
anchorage for large vessels in seven fathoms at the west end of White
Bay. Anchorages on the north side of the island are too exposed.

CHAPTER VIII

MARINA CAY

WE POWERED back between the Camanoes and ran along the lower shore of Great Camanoe to anchor fifty yards behind Marina Cay in four fathoms. This makes a fine anchorage in any kind of weather short of a gale. There is no pitch or roll in here and the sandy bottom makes excellent holding. Of course it is not as snug and landlocked as Trellis, but it affords privacy as well as excellent snorkeling along the reef which protects Marina Cay across the southerly approaches.

We took the dinghy in to a tiny beach-landing below the Robb White house. This was just a speck of beach where the rocks had been cleared and sand had washed in—and only enough of it for one dinghy at a time.

The Cay was then being leased by Bob and Nancy Scanlon who lived on St. Croix most of the time and sailed their little yawl the *Fancy Free* back and forth as the spirit moved them. Sometimes the Scanlons left a key over the door for the use of visiting yachtsmen but we found the house tightly boarded up with storm shutters and storm doors.

We had brought our snorkeling equipment and even a gunny sack in which to carry whatever we bagged back to *Renegade*. We wore tennis sneakers to walk along the knee-deep shallows to the outer edge of the reef. I happened to be walking ahead when I noticed I was in a sandy area that was covered with what appeared to me to be old conch* shells.

* Pronounced: conk.

"Someone must have dumped a load of old shells here," I remarked as I picked up a big one covered with gray, dead-looking moss. But the old conch was very much alive and the brown sickle-like claw which it uses for locomotion whacked out and tried to prod me. This gave me quite a start. When looking for conches it is well to remember that often in their natural state they take on a protective dull coloration. They look not at all like the shiny pink and white things tourists bring home from Florida to use for door stops. We picked up so many we had our sack full in half an hour. We had so many that we threw the small ones and the old tough-looking ones back into the sea and took a half sackful of medium ones around to the beached dinghy. Here we left Rufus ashore to clean them while we took the dinghy around the north side of the Cay and explored the eastern end of the reef there. There was nothing big enough to shoot for food on this little excursion, but we lingered for an hour over some submarine gardens of fan coral, tree coral, stag coral thoroughly alive with all kinds of small fish. Some of the fan coral has a tiny mollusk attached to it which is a pretty addition to any collection of shells. This is the Flamingo Tongue and when taken off the coral with the animal alive inside it can be cleaned to preserve the jewel-like enamel which is always dulled when the shell is found washed up on a beach.

Rufus showed us how he had processed the conches on the beach. You open the conch by knocking off the second point from the top. (A sharp whack with a hammer will do this.) In this hole you insert a sharp knife to cut the muscle which holds the animal secure in its shell. Now you can grasp the "sickle" and pull the white rubbery lump that is the conch body out of the shell. To clean this for eating you cut off the "sickle" and split the body with a knife, throwing away everything that isn't white.

There are many theories of cooking conch. Some say to beat it thoroughly to tenderize the meat before cooking. Others say cut it into small pieces and place in a pressure cooker of one-half sea water, one half fresh water, onions, bay leaf and cubed potatoes and heat at full pressure for one half hour.

We found that by using medium-sized conches the beating was unnecessary. We chopped the meat up fine and boiled it for twenty min-

Photo by Fritz Henle

The old sloop in the Sir Francis Drake Channel is one of the native craft which ply between the British and U. S. Virgins. The double ended ketch is a charter yacht out of St. Thomas.

utes. Then simmered it in butter, sliced potatoes and chopped onions in a frying pan until toasted thoroughly. This concoction was as delicious as anything we had ever eaten. And for once we had so much of the main entrée that Felix and Rufus admitted they were no longer hungry.

This night, after the boys had had their feast forward and had cleaned up the galley, they came back to the cockpit and sang a few calypso numbers for us. Rufus was the song-bird; Felix was very shy and just crouched on deck beside the dog house and hummed. Rufus' best number was "Oh de Sputnik's in de Sky" adapted from an old Trinidad ballad in which it is pointed out "Dat Columbus he din' need no dog to show him de way."

We were not particularly in the mood to be reminded of Sputniks but somehow Rufus' soft voice and unself-conscious rendering decontaminated the subject. After several very funny Sputnik verses Rufus concluded with that great Caribbean favorite "Brown Skin Gel— go home an' mine baybee."

Next morning after hot cakes, maple syrup and bacon we put on the sails and went out the channel on the north side of Marina Cay and once clear took a tack southeast that put Fallen Jerusalem right on our bow. We had about a fifteen knot wind and a clear blue sky overhead with popcorn clouds fringing the horizons north and south. This was again superb sailing and as we closed with Fallen Jerusalem we watched the blaze of the morning sun light up big and little isles, islets, rocks and islands all around us. There was Cooper blanketing off Salt and Dead Chest. And there was the other rock called Carvel. This Carvel from our angle looked like a freighter hull steaming through the pass between Cooper and Ginger. The PILOT says that this passage may be taken by steamers but sailing vessels are apt to be becalmed in the lee of Ginger. Beyond Ginger, to the east, is Round Rock Passage, the most eastern of the passages leading into Sir Francis Drake Channel. The PILOT says this is the best for vessels coming into the Channel from outside.

We had entered Drake Channel through this passage in 1956 when we sailed up the Windward-Leewards from St. Lucia. We had left St. Maartin in late afternoon and sailed through the night to find Round

Rock on our starboard hand at dawn, exactly the moment it was light enough to either see it or come about and sail off. It had been quite a thrilling experience to find that tiny landfall right on our nose after eighty-five miles of clipping along the same course at nine and ten knots. We learned later that this was as much luck as navigation.

I have collected a great many charts as the result of our voyages in different parts of the world and am always fascinated by curious names of islets and rocks. Groups of rocks will be called Hen and Chickens or Cow and Calves. Single rocks will be called Barrel o' Beef or Sail Rock or Carvel Rock. Some bear a striking resemblance to the animal or thing for which they are named. Many have not the remotest similarity. No doubt the ravages of time and weather are most often responsible for creating the discrepancies. A rock which reared up like a hen guarding her chicks a hundred years ago might today be so levelled off as to look more like a baby whale awash.

Fallen Jerusalem, however, looks to be exactly the thing its name implies. It can be instantly recognized from any direction. Here in miniature is the Holy City as subdued by Titus in 70 A.D. As we came closer we seemed to see a couple of adobe houses which the Roman Legionaires left intact. Even through the binoculars the strange rock formations looked more like part of a razed city than nature's handiwork.

CHAPTER IX

VIRGIN GORDA

CLOSE on our port hand we made out the rocks which mark the southern tip of Virgin Gorda. Next, to port, a white sandy beach. Then some scrub trees and rock rising gradually to the great slabs of granite which hide one of the really sensational sights to be seen in all the Virgins. Under these giant rocks are the Baths, so designated on H. O. Chart 3904 from British Surveys of 1848 and 1865.

To the left of the highest pile of rock slabs is a stand of fully grown coconut palms. I counted ten in all. They look like midgets next to the granite pile. Just to the left of the palms is the small very white sand beach where one lands to visit the Baths.

We anchored two hundred yards off the Baths in four fathoms with good sandy holding bottom. We were lucky that the seas were particularly calm this day. Often there is a heavy swell here that will roll the gunwales under. Be prepared to get out if a heavy ground swell starts, for you can get into trouble here.

At certain times one must use care going in to the beach. It is no place for an outboard because coral heads are near the surface close to the beach. The beach is rather steep and most dramatically framed by the topsy-turvy rocks on both sides. There was enough of a little surf running so we almost capsized landing. It is wise to carry your camera in a pressed-top paint tin for this kind of maneuver. If the tin gets away from you it will float and is easily retrieved.

Looking towards Tortola from the beachfront near the Baths the immediate scene has an unreal, Shangri-La quality which is evident in this picture. This day the seas were especially calm.

Notice how palm is dwarfed by the huge granite slabs of the Baths, Virgin Gorda. Entrance to the mysterious pools is just behind base of tree and requires crawling on hands and knees.

It was a walk of just a few yards to the coco-palms which guard the slabs which rise above them. The entrance seemed rather Egyptian, suggesting the colossal pillars of King Tut's time. We entered crawling on our hands and knees through the inverted V where two great slabs joined. Inside began a series of chambers filled with the clearest of water and lighted by shafts of sunlight which slanted in through a pattern of ceiling structure which would be any cubist's delight.

One outstanding characteristic was the feeling of purity of the place. It seemed alive and fascinating because of the play of diverted sunlight. But not a living thing was in the water. No moss, coral, sea urchins or fish. No birds nested in the rocky pinnacles. The place is so inaccessible for tourists that there was not a cigarette wrapper, a coke bottle or a footprint anywhere to indicate that it was part of this world.

Swimming in one of these pools is the strangest of sensations. It is pleasant and cheering and not eerie like the caves on Norman. Everything is so absolutely still and beautiful and the water so clear that one feels suspended in space. As we floated contentedly looking up at the awesome structure over our heads we wondered what sort of natural upheaval had played such tricks here. We also wondered just how secure everything was above us. There must have been a gentle earthquake to cause this for a violent one would have broken the great rocks into fragments. They were placed one on top of the other the way a child might deliberately balance a higgledy-piggledy lot of building blocks to show that they will stand without necessarily being piled up according to the book of instructions.

A further amazing thing about this great pile is that it continues down into the sea outside the Baths. Our diving glasses revealed what appeared to be the beginning of a whole palace of mysterious rooms below the surface of the sea. This area was well populated with fish of all sizes and colors who no doubt avoided the chambers above because no living coral grew there.

Rufus had swum down and turned the Danforth over, following our latest ritual. So we were well dug in and the boys had to really sweat it out on the windlass to get us out of there.

Sailing north for our next anchorages in Gorda Sound we passed two small white beaches with some coconuts which we were later told

Inside the Baths strangely vaulted ceilings break up the shafts of sunlight which penetrate from outside. The Baths are so inaccessible that only an occasional yachting party ever visits them.

were under option to the Rockefeller interests to be eventually the location of a large hotel. If Mr. Rockefeller has really sewn up all the places pointed out to us as his, the Virgin Islands may one day be known as the Rockefellers. (See Chapter XVII)

Next we sailed past the two mile long beach of St. Thomas Bay along which a reef runs near shore most of the way. We could see some of the red-roofed houses of Spanish Town behind the southern extremity of the hollow bay. There is an entrance around the north end of the reef where small native boats enter. The controlling depth of this pass is about six feet. We could see a little pier off Spanish Town with a couple of sloops anchored near it. A yacht can find a good anchorage off the pass in about five fathoms with good holding ground of sand. But this whole place is subject to big rollers from the north making it quite untenable at times.

We passed Colison Point and drew a bead on Mountain Point, the northwesternmost tip of Virgin Gorda proper. The PILOT calls this western side of Virgin Gorda *Western Roads* and, because of its protection to the northwestward by the Dog Islets, recommends it as an anchorage for large vessels well off shore in thirteen fathoms. The PILOT warns that in the winter months there is often a heavy ground swell but "Here with good ground tackle and a long scope of cable, there will be nothing to fear, as the rollers are seldom accompanied by much wind."

Between Colison Point and Mountain Point we felt the loss of breeze due to Virgin Peak rising thirteen hundred seventy feet above us. We passed a procession of bays within the big bay, with notches of sandy beach showing. Savana Bay, Pond Bay, Tetor Bay, Plum Bay, Trunk Bay and Long Bay slid by.

As we approached closer to Mountain Point and had a good view of the tiny cays to port called Seal Dogs, we noted that the right hand cay looked like the caricature of a man's head looking straight up in the air with a sharp pointed nose à-la-Steinberg.

After rounding Mountain Point we soon had Mosquito Island abeam, then Mosquito Rock, and we headed east by south for the entrance to Gorda Sound. This is a good place to spread out Chart No.

0569 *West Indies Virgin Islands Approaches to Gorda Sound.* This is a large-scale version of the area showing clearly the reefs to be contended with on either hand. There are no nuns or cans here and one must rely strictly on the eye.

The PILOT says the approach is dangerous at night and that vessels should time their arrival to daylight. From a distance the approach looks easy. There is Mosquito Island on your starboard hand—a prominent islet three hundred feet high and thirteen hundred yards in extent. On your port hand, some eighteen hundred yards to the eastward, is Prickly Pear Island two hundred fifty feet high and almost a mile long. This is the tranquil picture from a distance. But as you close in and aim for the center on a 170° course you begin to see the teeth and claws of the reefs. Coming at you from off to starboard is Colquhoun Reef which extends southeastward from Mosquito Island nearly twelve hundred yards. Coming at you from off to port is Cactus Reef which extends three hundred yards westward from the northwestern end of Prickly Pear Island.

Cactus Reef is steep-to and easily distinguished by the sea breaking over it; therefore it is best to incline toward the edge of it passing the end of the surf line some fifty yards off.

GORDA SOUND

The PILOT sums up Gorda Sound as "an excellent and capacious harbor." It is also beautiful, remote, and has some of the same magical quality we found in Norman's Bight. Here is a one mile wide by two miles long blue lake sheltered from all winds and rollers.

We took off sail and first powered into Biras Creek in the southeast corner of Gorda Sound. There is plenty of depth everywhere here except for unmarked Oyster Rock one hundred fifty feet off the southern shore. The rock has only two feet of water over it—a real booby trap. We went to the head of Biras Creek, a very cozy place with a thick growth of mangroves lining it at the water's edge all around. Here was excellent holding in three fathoms and, in short, the idyllic anchorage of all time . . . except for one thing . . . mosquitoes. Swarms of these devils boarded us and after we powered around to anchor in the lee of Saba Rock we closed up the boat and D.D.T.'d everything below and smeared ourselves with insect repellent.

Saba Rock is small, only fifteen feet high and protected to windward by a maze of reefs. We had found good holding in three fathoms about fifty yards inside the rock. A good breeze blew in from the Atlantic here and we experienced no further mosquito troubles. Here again, however, the cantankerous anchor landed wrong side up and Rufus dove down and turned it over.

We had had a long day. It was swims, two cocktails, dinner and everyone in his bunk by 7:30 P.M.

Next morning we were all up early and loaded the dinghy for an all-out expedition to the reefs outside Saba Rock. *Skipperkey* got wildly excited about the prospects of going ashore and jumped into the dinghy and paced it restlessly before we had finished our breakfasts.

When we landed on the little patch of sand at the rock *Skipperkey* raced around the shore and finally decided to sit it out near a clump of cactus and watch us as we fanned out in the immense coral garden stretching toward the outer reef.

We thought we had seen a great many fish up to this point. But we had in fact seen few compared with the teeming waters off Saba Rock. First off I found some odd floating leaves drifting aimlessly in the shadows. But when I tried to pick the leaves up they all swam off. These, the leaf fishes, are as odd as anything that swims.

Felix, Rufus and Eunice each shot pan-sized groupers in one, two, three order. By now we were in about eight feet of water and schools of sergeant majors, angel fish, triggerfish, squirrelfish, and butterfly fish were all around us. Next, a snort from Rufus and we joined him to see something that at first glance put our respective hearts in our throats. I had said of the tarpon at Norman Island that they were the largest things I ever hoped to see in the water. Here, close enough to touch, was a ten-foot shark lying on the bottom below us. This was not the long thin type but had a body, behind its blunt nose, as big around as a cow. On second glance we saw it was harmless.

I hadn't realized until this cruise that shark species vary as much in their degrees of ferocity as animals. This was a nurse shark which is indeed the cow of the shark family. They look like something out of a nightmare but are completely docile. According to the fish books nurse sharks often come in to sandy shallows and lie on the bottom at mating time. Sometimes they will lie in such shallow places that their dorsal fins are high out of the water. According to Breder's, FIELD BOOK FOR MARINE FISHES one can enjoy an exhilarating ride by grabbing their pectoral fins and straddling their backs prepared to dismount quickly as the shark reaches deep water.

Even though I was in possession of all this consoling information I was startled when Rufus dove down and jabbed the thing's tail with the end of his spear. As said often before in this narrative, the water is very, very clear; it even seems clearer than the atmosphere above it.

The shark's beady little eyes looked at us without changing expression. Slowly the huge body turned, the tail churned up a little cloud of sand and she moved away. The whole thing was like watching a movie in slow motion. But she didn't go far and it was very easy to follow her around. We repeated the business of prodding and watching several times before wearying.

Hazel and I were along purely as observers and did none of the shooting. Soon, however, we had a dozen fish on a string hanging from my inflated mattress. Since these tended to leave a trail of blood in the water I decided it would be prudent to put them on top of the mattress rather than risk attracting one of the shark family known as not-so-docile.

Eunice and the boys spread out farther on their hunt, and Hazel continued along as observer. I dropped back arranging the fish and treading water to admire the seascape up topsides for a change.

The usual flock of pelicans was diving in the shallows back toward *Renegade*. Several boobies were gliding fairly close by. I had read in novels of the South Seas how the under plumage of white sea birds reflect "the pellucid green of the lagoon shallows as they glide low over the atolls of the Pacific." I had seen this phenomenon once or twice when we were cruising through the islands beyond Tahiti. Now I was apparently in a spot where the angle of the sun in relation to where I was treading water was just right. A half dozen boobies glided low near me and not only their white breasts but the brown under plumage of

This is our anchorage at Gun Creek, in Gorda Sound. Rufus was an accomplished hand with sail palm and needle and is here working on a wind scoop for the forward hatch.

Hazel pauses to chat with Oswald Joseph and a pair of his friends above Gun Creek anchorage, Gorda Sound. Between the pier and *Renegade* four Tortola sloops swing to their moorings.

their wings changed to green a few feet above the water. The pelicans came nearer and though their bodies and the underside of their wings are all brown they too turned a bright green.

It was a lovely sight and as they circled in closer I thought to myself "These birds really like me. Wouldn't it be wonderful to speak the language of birds and have them for friends. To be a sort of St. Francis to the sea birds, so to speak."

I wasn't long on this tack of romancing when suddenly a booby made a long gliding pass coming down within a foot of the top of my head. Others followed and then six pelicans. It was not the St. Francis in me that was attracting all these feathered friends. It was the neat little pile of fish lying on top of the mattress. The next time they started to buzz me I went into my somewhat rusty Australian crawl and kicked up such a commotion pushing the mattress before me that the birds banked off and returned to their diving grounds.

Eunice and the boys were not shooting just for fun. The bag of a dozen one and two pounders provided a delicious lunch for all the ship's party, including *Skipperkey* who welcomed the change from the usual canned horse meat diet. There was enough left over to make a fish chowder for supper.

GUN CREEK

There is a bight called Gun Creek near the southwest corner of Gorda Sound. We powered over in the afternoon and anchored fifty yards off a small cement pier in about four fathoms with a bottom of mud and sand. There were three old native sloops moored near us. The hills rise high behind the pier and a small creek goes in past the pier to where several shacks stand.

Hazel and I took the dinghy ashore and walked up the hill a way to make some pictures of the anchorage. In this present-day world of motor highways everywhere, it is strange to be on an island with some thirty miles of shore front and not a single road of any kind. There are only donkey trails, rocky and unkempt; barely wide enough for either an animal or a person to pass.

Shortly after we left the pier a young lad, who said his name was Oswald Joseph, became our self-appointed guide and showed us a small schooner being careened for bottom painting on the bank of the muddy creek. He said most of the village was over a pass on the hill above us. The people raise a few cattle and also do some fishing for a livelihood. One neat little building stood half way up the hill. This, Oswald said, was the Methodist Church and once a month the Rev. Mullings comes over from Tortola to hold a service. A new storage tank had been built next to the church and an inscription had been scratched into the cement reading: "This cistern was built by Charles Wilfred Kuntz a True Son of the Soil." There was a notice board posted on a fence picket by the donkey path leading by the church. This was evidently the town square. Eleven official holidays were listed on the board for the year, including Empire Day, Colony Day, Sovereign's Birthday, Prince Charles' Birthday, and St. Ursula's Day (October 21).

There was also a notice warning all citizens of the British Virgin Islands that if they violate their permission to visit the U. S. Virgins by overstaying their thirty day privilege they will be subject to prosecution. Two recent violators of this law were given one year each in confinement. During the war when labor was scarce in St. Thomas the U. S. authorities tended to wink at this law. All natives of the outer islands would do three times as much work as the pampered protégés of Uncle Sam. But today, with a great many hard working Puerto Ricans entering the U. S. Virgins, the labor market is tight and the law strictly enforced.

We sat on the steps of the little church and wished that for a few moments we might push the calendar back some three hundred sixty-three years. For a whole week in early November of 1595 a fleet of twenty-seven ships and twenty-five hundred men commanded by Sir Francis Drake and Sir John Hawkins lay in the large landlocked harbor at our feet. It was here in Gorda Sound that a council of war was held on Drake's flagship *Defiance* and battle plans drawn for the attack on San Juan.

Drake had sailed from England in late August, with the Queen's blessing, on a scheme to bring an army to Nombre de Dios at the Isthmus and march across to sack Panama City and seize the treasure awaiting convoy to Spain. Just before he sailed, Elizabeth had received intelligence that a large ship of the Spanish gold fleet lay in San Juan harbor for repairs, following a dismasting in a gale off Puerto Rico. Drake and Hawkins were to make a surprise attack on San Juan and transfer the millions in gold from the treasure ship to their own hulls before proceeding to Panama.

On the night of November 11th Drake led the fleet through the Virgins via the channel now named for him. To have been a reporter with the proper credentials to meet Drake and interview him aboard his flagship at the moment in history before he sailed from Gorda Sound would have provided one of the greatest of interviews. Both Drake and Hawkins sickened and were buried at sea during this expedition which was a series of disasters from November 11th onward.

A visit with Drake in Gorda Sound would have caught the Admiral at the height of his career with a long series of amazing successes behind him. He had revolutionized the British concept of sea warfare. He was the first Englishman to use the Royal Navy as an instrument of attack rather than defense. He had in years past personally hijacked enough plunder from the ships of Philip of Spain to fill the treasury of England. He was the outstanding captain in the defeat of the Spanish Armada. He had circumnavigated the globe and on his return in the *Golden Hind* Queen Elizabeth I herself had come aboard to confer the knighthood.

Oswald Joseph walked back to the pier with us and pointed out a pathetic little graveyard where several slabs of concrete had been lettered in commemoration of the dead. On a tiny one for a small child a wreath of faded paper flowers hung over a small cross. The paper flowers vividly pointed up the bare poverty of this soil where few flowers are grown.

We returned to the rugged beauty of our anchorage behind Saba Rock and the boobies and pelicans. We were just in time to tune in on the 5 P.M. radio round-up.

Most yachts in the eastern Caribbean are equipped with radio telephones and at the appointed hours of 8 A.M., noon and 5 P.M. anyone with a message to be relayed can usually complete a call. The system works almost too well and, like several farmers on a party line, everyone knows everyone else's business.

The yacht call letters for the area appropriately enough all begin with the letter W which is Whiskey. *Renegade's* is (WK) Whiskey Kilo 3364.

"Hello *Renegade,* Hello *Renegade,* Hello *Renegade.* This is the *Squally,* Whiskey Hotel 3352 calling the *Renegade.*" (The 34 foot sloop *Squally* was in St. Thomas.)

"Hello *Squally,* Hello *Squally.* This is *Renegade,* Whiskey Kilo 3364 back to the *Squally.*"

"Where are you today Eunice? Can you get a message to Ed over on Beef. His batteries are down and we can't read him. Tell him *Thunderbird* is coming up from St. Kitts on. . . . (Interference—Hello *Sea Hawk,* Hello *Sea Hawk,* this is the *Porgy* calling the *Sea Hawk.*) . . . Hello *Porgy.* Can you stand by please until I complete this message to *Renegade?* (Silence) Do you hear me Eunice? Tell Ed that *Thunderbird* expects to be at Beef on Thursday and wants to get hauled on Friday. Do you read me Eunice—over."

"Hello *Squally—.* Yes I read you fine. We are anchored in Gorda Sound. We did not plan to stop at Beef on the way back but can if it's important. Over."

"*Thunderbird* says he has a sprung plank. Needs some caulking. Can you check with Ed about hauling him on Friday? Over."

"Alright, we'll check with Ed and talk to you tomorrow night at 5. Anything else? Over."

"No. And unless you have something further this is the *Squally,* Whiskey Hotel 3352. Off and clear with the *Renegade.*"

Listening in on this sort of thing is not the best way to relish the remoteness of a far away anchorage. It is nice, however, to know that all this service is at hand for an emergency. Besides all of the pairs of ears on yachts there are so many alert hams sprinkled around the islands that no message goes by unheard.

Eunice told us an amusing story about some friends of hers who own a 40 foot motor boat, *The Flying Saucer.* They were recently on the air testing a new transmitter.

"This is *The Flying Saucer.* This is *The Flying Saucer* testing. I would like a check with any one reading me. This is *The Flying Saucer* testing."

The message was immediately picked up by a ham operator in St. Croix who answered breathlessly, "Hello *Flying Saucer,* Hello *Flying Saucer,* I can hear you but I can't see you. Where are you? What are you? Over."

"This is *The Flying Saucer,* a 40 foot power cruiser. We are in the Sir Francis Drake Channel. Over."

The ham sighed and uttered just one word: "Oh."

The best thing regularly on the air is the weather broadcast at 6:55 A.M. each morning. This originates with the Coast Guard in Puerto Rico and concludes invariably with the lovely poetic sentence "There are no indications of a tropical disturbance in the Eastern Caribbean this morning." Old hands abbreviate this statement to NITDITEC.

Next to our great attachment for Norman Bight I would say we liked our anchorage off Saba Rock, between Prickly Pear and Biras hill. Gorda Sound would be a great place to bring children on a long vacation and turn them loose with sailing dinghys. There are few places in the world as ideally suited for small boat racing. There is also a good anchorage just below where Cactus Reef joins Prickly Pear. There is two and a half fathoms here just off a small beach of yellow sand.

We had about a fifteen knot breeze directly from the east the morning we sailed out the pass headed north for Anegada Island. We passed Necker Island about a mile north of Prickly Pear and agreed with the PILOT DIRECTIONS that there is nothing inviting about Necker or the body of water called Virgin Sound that lies between. There are a great many reefs and shoals hereabouts.

CHAPTER X

ANEGADA ISLAND

In an hour and a half we were off Ruffing Point on the west end of Anegada, which is Spanish for "inundated." The bleak and uninviting island looks low enough to be easily overwhelmed by the surrounding sea. Anegada is nine miles in length east and west, covered with low scrub and at no point is it higher than thirty feet above sea level. No wonder the peasants who live there are rugged individualists. Norman Fowler picked probably the toughest place on earth to start his shark meat cooperative. There are reefs and coral heads all around Anegada and at West End, where the approach is clearest, we could get no nearer than three-fourths of a mile from shore. Off the other end of Anegada is Horse Shoe Reef, one of the most dangerous areas for shipping in the world. The Pilot, always prone to understatement, calls this area, "a most dangerous reef upon which many vessels have been lost." Horse Shoe Reef extends southeastward for eight miles and from here south there is another foul patch of almost five miles of scattered coral heads which join up with Herman Reefs, another place strewn with the bones of wrecked ships. There is the hulk of a large steamer resting on Herman Reefs today. (See Chapter XVII)

When I mentioned earlier that it was probably as much luck as navigation—the night we crossed Anegada Passage and picked up Round Rock right on our nose at dawn—I did not mean to leave the subject there. We were sailing with Don Clother, one of the crack pilots of the Caribbean. The yacht was the 56 foot ketch *Electra II,* owned by Bob Crytser of St. Thomas. Bob also owned *Electra I,* which he called *Little Electra. Little Electra* was an almost new 45 foot all teak yawl. It was from Sparkman and Stephens designs and had been built for Bob in Japan. It was beautifully put together and even had oriental carvings in the main saloon.

Just a month after Don had made the perfect landfall with us he was bringing *Little Electra* up the islands and attempted the same crossing. For crew he had Murray Burt, another crack charter skipper who had made the crossing of Anegada Passage many times.

It was a very dark night and it was blowing hard. Just as they were changing watches at 4 A.M. there was a terrific grating, crunching sound and *Little Electra* rolled on her side. Then a swell hit her and knocked her over on her other side and pitched her over the reef into deeper water. Don and Murray guessed right away that they were on Horseshoe Reef, and indeed they were. Some twenty miles north of where they should have been. As they tell the story, it all happened so fast that they had no time to be scared. They got the sails down and put two anchors over within minutes. The luckiest thing for them was that they had been lifted high enough by the timing of the swell to be carried across the barrier in one bounce without opening up the bottom. They were bowling along at top speed and if they had hit when *Little Electra* was in a trough she would have been holed instantly to slide back off and sink in five fathoms before they could have unlashed the dinghy. Not that the dinghy would have been much use in the confused seas and maze of coral all around.

When morning came the wind had fortunately eased and the swell was down. But the outlook was thoroughly NG. Along the outer side of the reef for miles, seas were breaking. And on the inner side, coral heads completely surrounded the little pot hole where *Electra* lay.

The first person to hear Don on the radio telephone was Bob Crytser back in St. Thomas. He chartered a plane and was over the scene by 9 A.M. The weather was good and there was no immediate danger, but the big question was how to ever get *Little Electra* clear. From the air the yacht looked as hopelessly hemmed in as though she were in an ice pack in the Arctic Circle. Bob dropped a package of steaks to the boys and also a message to hang on until he could go back to St. Thomas and get some dynamite. Bob was back in the early afternoon and based himself on Anegada, two miles away, to begin salvage operations. Small native boats were available to get to *Electra* and carry the dynamite and percussion gear. For three days the blasting went on until at last the yacht was free. When she sailed into St. Thomas harbor a lusty cheer went up from the assembled yachts at Yacht Haven. According to the records, as far back as they have been kept, two hundred forty-seven vessels have foundered on Horseshoe Reef. *Little Electra* is the only craft ever to have gone in there and come out again.

We brought *Renegade* about and, as a Burton Holmes Travelogue would put it, "Bid goodbye to the little isle of Anegada."

It was a glitteringly bright day with a gentle roll and the good breeze continued from due east as we sailed past all the Dog islands. As the Dogs slid by to port, first the Seal Dogs, then George Dog with Great Dog behind it; then Cockroach, then West Dog, we were chattering so much about dogs that *Skipperkey* began running around the deck barking. Like a great many highly bred canines *Skipperkey* knows enough words to sometimes follow a conversation.

Cockroach is a forbidding looking rock, but as we passed we could see a nice little beach on the western shore of Great Dog. We discussed at some length, the idea of anchoring at Great Dog, accompanied by more barking from *Skipperkey*. But the breeze was just right for the big genoa so we put it on and succumbed once again to the pure delight of sailing. We were on course 230° headed for Scrub Island and we only had to trim in the jenny slightly to make it and point for Marina Cay. The sun was so bright that the bare, rocky eastern end of Scrub Island seemed to have a gash in it, just above the water, which looked like a cave. This turned out to be merely shadow caused by the intense sunlight. We rounded to at our old anchorage behind Marina Cay and had lunch. Not wanting to go into Trellis and say our goodbyes all over again we sent Felix over in the dinghy with a note about the hauling appointment for *Thunderbird*. Meanwhile I swam in to Marina Cay and picked up two dozen more conchs. We hadn't seen many frigate birds on the voyage and I was surprised to see one gliding a few yards over me as I was conching. He was truly gliding for he kept in the same

Photo by Sam Falk

In this view from the top of Bordeaux Mountain the camera is pointing Northeast with Tortola showing at upper left. In the foreground is Fortberg Hill. Just beyond it is Hurricane Hole.

position in the air riding the updrafts on the windward shore of Marina without flicking a wing. I consider frigates the most beautiful flyers of all birds. This one had perfect control of balance with only an occasional scissoring of his long forked tail.

We had a cheery note from Ed as we weighed and headed south. Ed's radio telephone was now working, and he had talked directly with *Thunderbird*. After rounding The Bluff of Beef Island we again put on the genoa and had a glorious sail down Sir Francis Drake Channel with the south shore of St. John as our destination. This is truly downhill sailing and with her clean bottom *Renegade* pushed ten knots easily all afternoon. By five o'clock we were off Privateer Point, St. John, with Flanagan Island to port. I reflected on my unfortunate friends sitting at their desks, high above the streets of Manhattan, answering their phones and dictating their letters, with an hour to go until the mad rush underground to the old 6:02 with its jam-packed bar-car and long queue of flannel-suited customers.

We were so bursting with health and clean living and the sheer joy of freedom that we broke into song. Fl, A, Double N, I,—G,A,N. spells Flanagan, we shouted. Then we attempted a soft rendering of Song of The Islands.

With the gathering dusk in the east the low gray bulk of Virgin Gorda at the far end of Drake Channel looked for the first time as the old Spaniard must have seen her when he called her the fat Virgin. On the right her head looked upward, with hair flowing beyond it. Her breast and large stomach were clearly defined, and it looked as though a blanket were over her from below her breast all the way to her feet some miles to the left. I remembered the remark of an old man we had overheard on the pier at Cruz Bay. "Dat Gorda gel so big, big, big, you say dar de virgin seven month wid chile."

HURRICANE HOLE

As one can see on the chart, Coral Bay is larger and offers better protection than St. Thomas Harbor. Some Danes thought Coral (Craal) Bay should be the chief harbor of the Danish West Indies. One Christian Martfelt, a Dane who visited the islands in 1765, said of

Craal Bay: "It is the best bay in the entire West Indies . . . It is twice as deep as any and can hold twice as many vessels."

Inside Coral Bay is Round Bay, almost a mile across; then deep inside is Hurricane Hole and its string of tiny bights.

I had long wanted to see Hurricane Hole. The name intrigued me. In island cruising one is frequently thinking, "Now where would we go if we were in for an all-out hurricane?"

In my notes on Hurricane Hole is the remark: "Plenty of bights in here (no pun intended)." Deep inside is as good protection for yachts as anywhere in the islands. But the mosquitoes drove us out ten minutes after we had anchored. For a few minutes we considered a swim to get away from the blood-lusting pests. The water, however, was literally packed with large jellyfish of the stinging variety. They were as large as saucepans.

A couple of small houses were perched on the hills above us. Everything is steep-to here with no beaches, and mostly bush or rocks or mangrove roots at the water's edge. A man stepped onto the verandah of one of the houses and inspected us through his binoculars. He had a small speedboat tied up below his house, so we figured he must be one of the retired Americans at Coral Bay we had heard about. Like all retired Americans on an island he must have been terribly proud of his place and it seemed a shame to turn right around and go out as though we didn't like it.

As we powered out of Coral Bay we battened down all the hatches and had Rufus and Felix do a saturation job with the D.D.T. below. Still a few mosquitoes lingered around the cockpit until we got out into the breeze which was right on our bow as we left Flanagan to port and pointed for the caves of Treasure Point. We couldn't resist another night at Norman Island, just an hour away. It was almost sunset and a large harvest moon was already rising over Pelican Islet. Astern of us a spectacular sunset sky was in the process of making up.

By the time we were at anchor at our old stand in the Bight, the sky behind us over St. John was a mass of flaming reds with patches of soft blues and pinks showing between jagged lines of black and gray clouds of every wild shape imaginable. In October and November the sunset skys over the Caribbean are not to be matched anywhere in the world.

When the show in the west had faded away the full moon took over and made unusual shadows on the deck and in the cockpit. So bright was the scene it was easy to pick out the pelicans perched in the scrubby trees along shore.

In the cabin we found one lone mosquito who had resisted being snuffed out by the D.D.T. But he was groggy and we caught him with the fly swatter. It would have been outrageous to transport any of those Hurricane Hole devils to pest-free Norman. Sort of like doing a Captain Bligh in reverse.

We talked over our itinerary and decided we would visit Jost Van Dyke next day. And since to get there we would pass Little Thatch Island it would be fun to call on the American who was building there.

CHAPTER XI

LITTLE THATCH

Nᴇxᴛ ᴍᴏʀɴɪɴɢ we had a fine broad reach almost to Frenchman Cay, then ran another mile down The Narrows to the west tip of Little Thatch. Behind the white cement house, with a tower on the point, there was the scaffolding of another house going up. We took off the sails and powered in close and blew three blasts on our horn. We could see a workman climb down a ladder and walk toward the white tower, waving to us to come around behind the point where there is a landing beach. We powered around to a pretty little cove and idled the motor against the current while Rufus took a note in to Bob Fox, the American, asking him if he would like to sail to Jost Van Dyke with us. Soon a grinning rather chubby young man in his mid-thirties was alongside. Eunice had met him before in St. Thomas and made the introductions.

"Why don't you all come ashore and have a swim and stay for lunch?"

"We wanted you to come to Jost with us and have lunch aboard," said Eunice.

"Okay. I guess my boys will keep busy while I'm gone. I wanted to pay a call on the Princess anyway," said Bob as he climbed in over the transom and secured the dinghy painter.

Bob (for Burwell) Fox, had been busy building on Little Thatch for almost a year. He and his wife had come from the U. S., first to St. Croix seeking the peaceful island life. They liked St. Croix but grew to be intrigued with the Tortola area as they became more and more at-

Felix tosses the lead as Bob Fox brings *Renegade* in close enough to his domain at Little Thatch so as to swing clear of the strong current which runs through Thatch Cut.

Renegade sits at anchor off Little Thatch. West End, Tortola is to the right of her sticks and Little Jost Van Dyke is in the distance. Bob Fox's beach bar is beyond donkey.

tached to cooks and gardeners they hired who were Tortolans. This Tortola help could only work for them twenty-nine days at a time because of the law. One day their gardener told them there was some good beach property for sale cheap on Tortola, so Bob flew to St. Thomas and embarked on the *Youth of Tortola* to see for himself.

As the *Youth* started through The Narrows past Little Thatch, one of the ·passengers standing near the rail with Bob, turned to him and for no reason at all said: "That Little Thatch. That belong to me an' my six brothers."

"Do you want to sell it?"

"Yes, I sell, but I doan' know ef my six brothers wants to sell."

Bob never looked at the property on Tortola he had come to see, but started negotiations at once with the seven brothers. After months of finagling back and forth between St. Croix and Road Town, Bob nailed the deal down to the extent of signing an option agreement with the seven brothers. A man of lesser determination would have let the whole thing go somewhere along the line of frustrating negotiations. Other bidders got into the act as they heard about it, including a Rockefeller lieutenant. But the brothers liked Bob and stuck with him. Finally, when negotiations reached the stage of getting Crown permission for the purchase, the governing body in Antigua put up some new barriers. Bob had to guarantee that some $30,000 worth of improvements would go in within the first year and until then the government permission would be held in escrow by the Crown. Luckily Bob had a partner in the U. S. who was ready at the right moment to help him with adequate backing. In the meantime Bob's wife decided she didn't want to live on Little Thatch and they parted company. Bob didn't say what he and his partner had finally invested in his sixty acre island, but recently he was offered $125,000 for it and, although this represented a neat profit, he turned it down without even considering it. He is putting up four bungalows to rent to his stateside friends in the winter season and is booked solid for years into the future. (See Chapter XVII)

CHAPTER XII

JOST VAN DYKE

JOST VAN DYKE's Great Harbor was only an hour's sail from Little Thatch. Jost Van Dyke runs three and a half miles east and west and has one summit in the middle which rises over one thousand feet. There are three harbors on the southern shore, White Harbor, Great Harbor and Little Harbor. The PILOT does not recommend any of the harbors for other than small vessels. White Harbor is studded with reefs; Little Harbor should be entered carefully with a lookout posted for reefs, but, once inside, is snug, shoaling to four fathoms.

Only about two hundred natives live on the island and mostly engage in fishing or raising a few cattle. We wanted most to meet Bob's friend, the Princess, and she resided near the little cement pier at the head of Great Bay. Great Bay is a half mile square and free of hazards, shoaling to two fathoms fifty yards from the pier. This is where we anchored.

When we landed the dinghy alongside the pier we were met by a dozen curious children and a smiling old fellow in a pith helmet. When the old man offered to sell us two papayas for $1.00 Bob spoke up.

"How much did you say?"

"One dallah suh. She two fo' one dollah."

"Look, we're not tourists. We live here. Those things are worth 15 cents apiece."

"Yessuh," said the old man. "Dat's right suh."

Princess Alexandrine Sewer of Jost Van Dyke stands near the well that supplies the Methodist Church. The old foundations once supported the house where England's great Dr. Lettsom was born.

But on closer inspection the fruit was too ripe and quite worthless.

We had only walked a few yards west along the donkey trail that is Jost's main thoroughfare when we were met by a smiling little old woman who shook hands with Bob warmly.

"Well, well Mistah Bob; how come you stay away so long?"

"Princess, I have been very busy but I really mean to come over and see you regularly. Meet my friends."

We shook hands with Princess Alexandrine Sewer, part of the illustrious Sewer family of St. John. Princess Alexandrine ushered us a few yards farther along the road to a small shack of plaster and wattle that had recently acquired a fresh coat of royal blue paint. Inside was a table and a few chairs, a counter with some canned goods on it and a kerosene-run "fridge." All was clean if somewhat disordered. She told us to help ourselves out of the ice box and we each had a beer. After we had cooled off and exchanged compliments, we were invited into the little house next door and had a very pleasant visit with a truly remarkable woman.

When Princess Alexandrine's husband had died some thirty years before, she was left with nine children (five girls and four boys) and a couple of head of cattle. Starting from there she got her little store going and acquired a few more cattle. She managed to bring up all the children and see them through such schooling as was available at the Methodist Church next door and also in St. Thomas. Her livestock holdings grew until she owned most of the cattle on Jost Van Dyke. She also owned Little Tobago Island and leased it to a man who was raising goats there.

Most of her children and twenty grandchildren live in the Bronx and Brooklyn and they have always been good about writing. Once they all got together and paid her way up for a visit. The walls of her very tidy living room were lined with greetings from her children and grandchildren. There were many Christmas scenes of snow and icicles and several satin pollows with Mother's Day inscriptions on them. One of the pillows was from Panama and one from the Philippines. These were from sons Link and George who were in the U.S. Navy and Army respectively. Link's whole name, she told us, is Grand Duke Lincoln Cromwell Sewer, but he took such a ribbing in the Army that he changed it to just plain Link. George was baptised King George Emanuel, but prefers being called George by his Navy pals.

Princess Alexandrine was a devout woman and had a well-worn bible on the parlor table and another on the counter of her store. She took us next door and showed us the church which is used on weekdays as a school. She said it was nearly destroyed in the hurricane of 1916. On that calamitous occasion the roof blew all the way to St. John.

She showed us some old foundation stones and said that there was originally a "big white folks house" where the church now stands. It was her impression that the great William Thornton once lived here. William Thornton has also been claimed as a Tortola great. In a little pamphlet called *A History of Tortola,* which I had picked up in Road Town, William Thornton is described as a Tortola boy who began his career as a self-taught amateur architect. In 1792 he learned from a visiting shipmaster that there was a competition then being held to choose a design for the new Federal Capitol building in Washington, D. C. Thornton decided to compete and quickly made some drawings and went to Philadelphia, the temporary Capitol, only to learn that the competition had already been closed.

Neither President Washington nor Thomas Jefferson, however, liked any of the fourteen elaborate entries which had come in and when they saw Thornton's they were greatly impressed. They asked the commissioners to reconsider all the other plans against the new one. Of the Thornton plan Jefferson said "simple, noble, beautifully and excellently arranged."

Thus William Thornton of the British Virgin Islands won the $500. prize and also a choice lot in the new city. He became a close friend of Washington, and in 1802 the President appointed him the first commissioner of patents, a post he held until his death in 1828.

Thornton may have had a house on Jost Van Dyke. But it is more likely that the ruins under the church were the remains of a Great House where another famous Virgin Islander was born. Several books record the birth of John Coakley Lettsom as having taken place on Jost Van Dyke, November 22, 1744. Lettsom's people were wealthy sugar growers. He was sent to school in England at twelve and at sixteen he was apprenticed to an apothecary in Yorkshire. He was the founder of

the Medical Society of London and became known as the most distinguished English physician of his day. In 1767, when he was given the
news that he had inherited the vast family estate on Tortola, his first
act was to sail to the islands and free the several hundred slaves law-
fully his.

Lèttsom was very popular in England and had a keen sense of humor.
He liked to refer to himself as the "Volatile Creole" and he was personally responsible for the oft-quoted bit of doggerel:

> I John Lettsom
> Blisters bleeds and sweats 'em
> If in spite of this they die
> I John Lettsom

Princess Alexandrine walked to the pier with us and said she was
going to sail over and call on Bob one day. The man with the over-ripe
papayas was on hand again to bargain with us but she shooed him off.

Papayas are called paw paws in these islands and their properties
for tenderizing meats were known long before Adolf's Tenderizer was
invented. The Princess asked us if we liked the green paw paw cooked
as a vegetable. We hadn't tried this but Bob said it is delicious.

The paw paw is such an incomparable digestive that there are many
legends about the fruit. The more superstitious natives believe that
if a goat is tied to a paw paw tree for five days before it is slaughtered it
is tenderized by some process of osmosis of the atmosphere. There is the
story of the rich planter who suffered so badly from acute indigestion
that he ordered his servant to cut the biggest paw paw he could find
each day and place it on a shelf over his master's bed each night. The
third night of this treatment a wind blew through the shutters with
such violence that the paw paw rolled off its shelf and dropped into
bed beside the dyspeptic planter. In the morning, as there was no
answer when the servant knocked at the bedroom door, he entered and
to his surprise found only the paw paw in the bed. The master had
vanished and was never again seen. When the paw paw was opened the
planter's false teeth, signet ring and three pyjama buttons were recovered.

JOST VAN DYKE

As we sailed out of Great Harbor bound for Little Thatch, Bob pointed to Sandy Cay, about a half mile off the southeastern tip of Jost Van Dyke.

"Another one of Mr. Rockefeller's recent acquisitions," he said.

"Another hotel do you think?"

"I don't know. It's a pretty little islet with sandy beaches almost all round. Maybe he is going to give it back to the British for a park. Mr. Rockefeller recently bought several hundred acres on the top of Tortola and deeded it back to the island. There is a stand of virgin timber up there that he was anxious to preserve. That is the only area which wasn't brought under cultivation in slave days."

Through the binoculars we could see the silhouettes of some of the great trees near the peek of Mount Sage nearly two thousand feet above us.

On the chart Sandy Cay, Green Cay and Little Jost Van Dyke seem to enclose a nice anchorage area. But there is a lot of foul ground here and the best way to explore it for snug anchorages is with a shoal-draft boat. There is a fair temporary anchorage off the west end of Sandy Cay.

As we approached Thatch Island Cut on our return, Bob said the remains of an old pirate fort lay in behind Belmont Point near Tortola's West End. There is a seventeen hundred acre estate there owned by an Englishman who bought it in 1914 for thirty-five cents an acre.

On our starboard hand was Great Thatch Island, about a mile and a half long east and west and rising to six hundred feet at its highest point. Bob said it was recently sold for $150,000.

Renegade could feel the grip of the five knot current as we entered Thatch Island Cut. The PILOT says that sailing vessels should not attempt the Cut from the northward "except with a southward current, as the eddies and currents are very strong."

I asked Bob if he were sitting here in a rowboat without oars, where would he drift.

"All the way to St. Thomas today. Yesterday all the way to Road Town."

In behind the northeast end of Little Thatch is Sopers Hole with the little village of West End flanking it on the Tortola shore. "Sopers

Hole is deep enough and large enough to hold a battleship," said Bob.

We thought Sopers Hole was undoubtedly named for some pirate or former governor named something like Wilburforce J. Soper. But the soper is a small bait-fish. Boat loads of sopers are often netted here.

Off Bob's beach we found good holding in three fathoms, away from the stream of current.

We all ate aboard and then went ashore. The view from the tower room where Bob slept was one of the best in the islands. From his bed he could watch every vessel passing through The Narrows and see islands all the way to Puerto Rico.

When the building program is completed on Little Thatch we think it will be one of the nicest places to stay in the Caribbean. We had a swim before taking off and learned something about salt water soap that will interest any sailor. Bob reached up on top of a big boulder by the beach and took down a small bottle which he tossed to me.

"Try that for salt water lather," he said. "But don't use too much or you'll make a bubble bath out of my swimming hole."

I poured a little of the yellow liquid in my hand and passed the bottle back. It was the only detergent I had ever tried in salt water that really lathered as though the water were out of a rain barrel.

"That's Halo, that stuff all the singing commercials are about in the States. A fellow in Road Town ordered ten bottles of it and someone got the cyphers in the wrong place and one thousand came down here. So everybody bought it by the case, cheap. I accidentally discovered it works in salt water and use it every day when I swim."

By sunset *Renegade* was back at anchor in Cruz Bay, St. John, and we were having cocktails with the Fords. The little settlement was about to experience something new in tourism to further rock them back on their heels. The *Kungsholm* was due to anchor at Caneel Bay next morning and would be the first cruise ship ever to enter these one-time tranquil waters.

CHAPTER XIII

CANEEL BAY

THE *Kungsholm* is not one of the largest ships in the world but at anchor in tiny Caneel Bay (also called Durloe Bay) it looked gigantic. Try to imagine a luxury liner sitting in the middle of Lake Winnepesaukee and you have something of the idea.

We went into Caneel Bay early and anchored near the dock, before any of the tourists went ashore. There seemed to be hundreds of people lining the rails of the *Kungsholm* as we passed. As *Renegade,* with her ensign fluttering over the stern, was mistaken for a welcoming party there was a great deal of waving and picture-taking from the decks above us.

The Caneel Bay complex proved to be the most costly operation for its size in the entire Caribbean. It was originally planned to accommodate only one hundred guests. A quick statistical highlight will indicate the magnitude of the enterprise. In one year, January to December, 1955, Mr. Rockefeller spent over $2,000,000 on modernization and rehabilitation alone. This was on top of the original purchase price for the six hundred and fifty acre estate containing ten of the finest beaches on St. John.

Here is a quote from a fact sheet, issued in December 1955 by Caneel Bay's New York headquarters in Rockefeller Center.

"Caneel Bay Plantation was first opened in 1930 as a small resort by the West Indies Company. After a succession of different ownerships it was offered for sale in 1952 by the Rhode Island Charity Trust and

A group of happy tourists waves to us from the stern rail of the flag-bedecked cruise ship *Kungsholm* just after she anchored in Caneel Bay for a precedent-shattering visit.

purchased by Mr. Laurance S. Rockefeller. All of the stock of Caneel Bay Plantation was given by him to Jackson Hole Preserve, Inc., and the improvements totaling over $2,000,000 have been made with personal funds given by Mr. Rockefeller. Any income received from the operation of the hotel facilities under such a lease or concession arrangement would continue to be used only to further the conservation purposes of Jackson Hole Preserve, Inc., including its activities in connection with the proposed Virgin Islands National Park."

About the plan for the National Park the prospectus has this to say:

"To preserve the primitive charm and unspoiled beauty of the island of St. John and make it available for the enjoyment of the public Mr. Laurance Rockefeller began the acquisition of lands on St. John in November, 1954, with the aim of ultimately turning over such holdings to the National Park Service for the establishment of a national park. More than 5,000 acres have been acquired through Jackson Hole Preserve, Inc., and a bill for the creation of the Virgin Islands National Park, the nation's 59th park, is now awaiting Congressional action. The proposed park would be limited to an area not exceeding 9,500 acres on St. John and adjacent rocks and cays. The park boundaries would skirt principal settlements of St. John and encompass two-thirds of the island's acreage."

Thus the two projects, Caneel Bay beach resort and the Virgin Island National Park, were interrelated from the start.

We inspected several of the row of beachfront rooms which look like a well-designed motel. They are built of native stone and stucco and are low and unobtrusively located behind a row of sea grape trees which grow out of the sand a few steps from the water's edge. The handsomely furnished rooms are small but one need never be indoors in such a lovely setting. A room here for two is $50.00 per day with meals in the winter season. The suites, that is living room and bedroom, are $60.00 per day. We also looked at two private cottages located separately from the beach rooms. One of these consisting of a living room and two bedrooms suitable for a couple with a child is $100.00 per day. The summer season rate between May 1st and December 1st is about one-third less.

Photo by Fritz Henle

The Caneel Bay Hotel beachfront rooms and dining lounge are almost hidden by sea grape trees at lower right. In center are the cottages. In the far distance is Jost Van Dyke.

A National Park Service guide explains to a visitor the workings of an eighteenth century sugar mill—one of the ruins on the old Danish Estate Annaberg, St. John.

A short distance behind the beach rooms are the ruins of the Great House and sugar mill which were in operation in the early 18th century when over one hundred plantations were flourishing on St. John. Here, one Peter Durloe lived. This was the Durloe for whom the Bay and Durloe Cays were named. The house figured prominently in the events following the abortive slave rebellion of 1733. On November 3rd of that year several slaves bearing fire wood made their usual morning call at the gate of Fort Berg located in Coral Bay. After the sentry let them in they carefully piled the wood on the ground and then pulled cutlasses out from under it and killed the entire garrison of seven men. An eighth soldier who was outside the fort at the time managed to spread the alarm and escape by sloop to St. Thomas to get help. As the slaves around the island got the word, the massacre of planters and burning of Great Houses commenced. Several of the planters who escaped the initial onslaught went to the Durloe estate and, thanks to the small arsenal Peter Durloe kept for such an emergency, they were able to resist until troops came from outside. Finally French troops from Martinique landed, and rather than be taken as prisoners the remnant of blacks not killed in the fighting jumped to their deaths over the bluff at Mary Point opposite Little Thatch. The most effective weapon was a small cannon which Durloe had previously mounted on his roof and had often used to take pot shots at pirate ships which approached too close to Caneel Bay.

The Durloe Great House is not in ruins today because of the slave revolt, but because with the abolition of slavery no planter could keep an estate going. When the planters departed, wind and weather gradually disintegrated any of the old palaces still standing.

St. John, like all the sugar islands is a place of memories. But not all of the memories are sordid ones. On December 1st, 1956, a celebration took place that St. Johnians will recall with a warm glow for many a year to come. On that date Mr. Rockefeller handed over to the U. S. the deed to the thousands of acres of parkland which he had acquired. He also put on a dinner at Caneel Bay Plantation for everybody on the island. The entire island population including the aged and infirm and tiny babies is seven hundred and twenty. They all came to dinner. Some traveled by donkey and some by boat. There were dignitaries

Photo by Sam Falk

The ruins of the old Great House at Caneel Bay is a focal point for tourists. This was the main stronghold defended by the planters during the slave rebellion of 1733.

Photo by Sam Falk

Part of the ruins of the original sugar mill at Caneel Bay, one of the 106 plantations which were flourishing in 1733 when the sugar islands were at peak prosperity.

This remarkable aerial photograph shows most of the north shore of St. John, looking east. Caneel Bay is right foreground. Next are Hognest Bay, Trunk Bay, and Francis Bay.

Photo by Fritz Henle

from New York and some two hundred visitors from the other islands. The *New York Herald Tribune* carried a story headlined "Nine Hundred and Twenty Get Barbecued Pig in Virgin Islands."

Andromeda Keating and her twin sister Myrah, headed up a battalion of women who ladled out the food as the long line marched past with plates in hand. The Keatings had cooked some five hundred pounds of meat in their outside ovens for the party. In addition, hams were baked and turkeys roasted by the chef at Caneel Bay Plantation. The two hundred pounds of pig was charcoal-broiled in St. Thomas and came over on the *Chocolate Queen*. Hundreds of cans of free beer were consumed. And, of course, barrels and barrels of the favorite drink of the islands, rum punch. After the speeches, the flag-raising, and the playing of the Star Spangled Banner, calypso bands took over and everybody danced.

We went back to *Renegade* just as the first launch loads of tourists were coming in off the *Kungsholm*. By 9 A.M. we were leaving Pillsbury Sound on a long tack south, expecting to tack back after a few miles and try once again for a landing at Reef Bay and a look at the Carib carvings. But the sea was even more boisterous than it was before and a landing at Reef Bay was quite impossible for anything smaller than an L.S.T. Reef Bay is open and reef-studded and no place to loiter with a keel boat on a boisterous day.

We tacked back in and when we were opposite the northern tip of Great St James Island we loosed the sheets and ran through Current Hole. This is a passage four hundred yards wide between Great St. James Island and St. Thomas. In the center of the passage Current Rock rises thirteen feet out of the water. By leaving it to starboard we were in a channel two hundred yards long with twenty-three feet of depth under us. A tidal current runs north and south through Current Hole at over three knots so here is no place to be caught with no wind and no motor. Five miles ahead of us was Buck Island with its white light tower prominent on its one hundred and twenty-five foot high peak. Buck Island is part of a cluster of small rocks called the Capella Islands and has long been a prominent landfall for vessels coming to St. Thomas. There is a small bight on the southwest shore of Buck Island where a wharf and boat landing is located.

Photo by Fritz Henle

Two yachts have come over from St. Thomas to anchor off the beautiful beach at Trunk Bay. This view is looking west from the site chosen by the Boulon family for their first house.

CANEEL BAY

As we left Current Hole channel we could see into the little bight on Great St. James called Christmas Cove. Eunice had always anchored at the cove for swims on previous cruises. The yacht set named it because of the custom of everyone rendezvousing there on Christmas Day. There is two fathoms with excellent holding bottom up to within ten yards of the sandy beach.

The sky was never bluer. The water was never bluer. The breeze was firm and steady out of the east. St. Thomas Harbor was an hour away. But we didn't want to go in. We wanted to keep sailing.

We had intended to spend a couple of days replenishing our supplies in St. Thomas before taking off for St. Croix. But we had done some shopping at Cruz Bay and now lacked nothing vital. St. Croix, sitting forty miles south on the horizon, looked especially close in the brilliant sunshine. With one voice we said "let's go." With the wind the way it was *Renegade* could easily make it to St. Croix in five hours.

As we headed south into some open-water sailing which is as fine as any to be had in this world, we got out the books on St. Croix. The island is largest of the American Virgins with an area of eighty-two square miles. Mount Eagle, rising over a thousand feet, is St. Croix's highest point and is easily picked out at the western end where the high land is. The island is nineteen miles long east to west, and five miles wide at its widest part. Aside from the high area at the west end, most of St. Croix is broad rolling valleys and scattered hills.

All of the Virgin Islands, with the exception of St. Croix, rise out of the sea from a great shelf called Virgin Bank which is eighty-five miles long and twenty-four to thirty-two miles wide.

St. Croix is separated from Virgin Bank by a deep crevasse on the sea bottom called Anegada Trough. Soundings in the Trough have recorded depths of more than two miles.

I remarked earlier that the sky was never bluer nor the water never bluer than when we started south. Perhaps it was just our imaginations, but we thought we found the water bluer over Anegada Trough.

It is generally believed that the sea takes on its hue as a reflection of the sky above. I have the authority of the late Harold (THE RAFT BOOK) Gatty, however, that the sea does not reflect the sky but gets its color from the chemical composition of the water. According to Gatty, whether the sea is blue or green depends mainly on the salinity. Because there is more evaporation, and thus more salt content in the waters near the equator, these waters are bluer. In the cool seas of the Arctic and Antarctic latitudes there is less evaporation and these waters are greener. Gatty says that the color intensifies as depths are greater, so perhaps our observation over Anegada Trough was not imagination.

I must confess that Mr. Gatty's theories rather confuse me. I have observed the ocean off Newport scores of times when we have sailed that area and the colors of the seas were very inconsistent. I have seen a morning sea that was very blue and an afternoon sea that was very green. I have seen many a gray sea which seemed to reflect the gray sky above.

CHAPTER XIV

ST. CROIX

St. Croix is unique of all the American Virgin Islands in that it has only one harbor. This is no doubt why it, rather than St. Thomas, was the seat of government for the Danish West Indies for so many years. With only one harbor to fortify, the island was practically impregnable to attack. Furthermore, this one harbor, Christiansted, is well fortified at its entrance with the natural protection of reefs and shoals.

Christiansted Harbor, on the north shore, about seven miles west of East Point, is easily recognized from the sea in daylight. The PILOT describes the anchorage as ". . . in a basin protected from the sea by Long Reef and Scotch Bank. A tortuous channel leads in behind the reef to the anchorage. The greater portion of the harbor is shoal. . . . The channel into the harbor is so intricate that strangers are advised to take a pilot and it should not be attempted at night without one. The turns are sharp and a vessel may have to drop anchor to assist in making them. It is dangerous for larger vessels to attempt to enter Christiansted Harbor during squally weather for if heavy squalls break while entering the ship may be caught in a dangerous position with the possible necessity of anchoring in a very narrow channel, with shoals on either side."

Of course the PILOT is concerned here with large vessels, not yachts and small craft. *Renegade* had been in before and had the necessary local information. In broad daylight in good weather any yacht can follow chart 935 and power in easily enough.

Photo by Kronfeld

In this view looking northeast above Christiansted, Hotel-on-the-Cay is in center with the reefs and shallows showing beyond. Trading vessels are at city dock, in the center of picture.

This old sugar mill which has been remodeled into a house is typical of several such conversions on St. Croix. The structures are surprisingly roomy inside, and they make very cozy guest cottages.

ST. CROIX

There are many prominent land marks in and around the town of Christiansted. The hills back of the town are all conspicuous and on one, Mt. Welcome, there is a stone tower and the remains of a sugar mill. Old Fort Christiansvaern and the white library building and a clock tower are all easily recognized near the water front.

The yacht skipper entering Christiansted harbor will first sight black buoy No. 1. This he will leave to port while he steers for the red and white radio tower of station WIVI on Fort Louise Augusta. The channel is well marked and deep, involving a sharp swing to starboard in sight of the fixed marker off the Fort. The channel leaves Round Reef to port and now heads for the fort in the town of Christiansted. Protestant Cay is rounded leaving it to starboard and the skipper proceeds west to the yacht basin. Protestant Cay is a small wooded islet about one hundred fifty yards north of town. It has an elevation of some forty feet. There had been several attempts to promote a large hotel on Protestant Cay. At the time of our visit there was a small one called Hotel on the Cay. It was in the center of the islet in a cluster of trees with a flag flying from its flagstaff on the roof. (See Chapter XVII)

After yachts pass between Protestant Cay and the dockside they find a good anchorage off the replica of a sugar mill which has been built at the pier of the Club Comanche.

We spent a week on the island and during this time there were never fewer than six yachts at anchor here. The Club Comanche hotel was owned and run by a couple of American yachtsmen, Ed Dale and Guy Reynolds. They kept their yacht *Comanche* at the anchorage there and it was generally available for charter. Yacht chartering throughout the Virgins was just beginning to develop into a major and lucrative industry.

Eunice had done her share of sightseeing on St. Croix on a previous call so she turned her attention to snorkeling the reefs off the cay. Hazel and I, in true busman's-holiday fashion, sought out the owner of the Tortola sloop, *North Star,* which takes day-sailing tourists to the local Buck Island, some five miles east and a mile and a half offshore. We packed a picnic lunch and as we waited on the pier for the *North Star* to pick us up were joined by an attractive young couple who were stay-ing at the Comanche and also had picnic lunches for Buck Island. Wil-

Bomba of Christiansted unravels a tangle of fish line as he steers *North Star* by leg pressure. The yacht anchorage and the Club Comanche "sugar mill" are in the background.

ton and Virginia Dillon lived in New York where he is an anthropologist with the Phelps-Stokes Foundation. This was their first visit to the Virgin Islands and they had flown to St. Croix for a week, after which they intended to see something of St. Thomas and St. John.

Bomba (the ancient term for slave foreman) was the jovial black skipper of the *North Star* and handled the heavy 30 foot museum piece with a nonchalant ease which was a delight to behold. Bomba is a purist who will have no traffic with motors and apparently needs none. The *North Star* is so cumbersome in coming about that Bomba uses his anchor for nearly every maneuver near shore. This is approved native practice and may be frequently seen as these craft come up to a dock. He sailed down wind until almost upon us at the Comanche pier. He cut quite a figure standing with his toes locked around the tiller and his white pith helmet on the back of his head. Just as *North Star*'s bow was a length off he kicked the helm over and lumbered casually forward to throw his anchor over. The anchor bit, the bow came up and the stern swung to us with inches between it and the pier. The big sails fluttered, we four stepped aboard, Bomba hauled the anchor up and again casually walked the length of the boat to wrap his toes around the tiller and then sheet in the sails for the tack out across the harbor. He missed several yachts by inches but the composed grinning expression on his face never changed. When we got into the channels where the reefs abound Bomba slumped into the cockpit with the helm under his armpit and almost went to sleep as he conned the *North Star* out to open water.

As may be gathered, Bomba is one of those local characters, colorful and independent, yet with the art of knowing the line between freshness and courtesy. In a region where all too many hands are outstretched for tourists' dollars, the guilessness of Bomba is a refreshing treat. It is no act; you can watch the man operate and be sure he is the genuine article. And happily, in justice to the human race, it pays off. Bomba is probably the best-tipped boat hand in the Caribbean.

Half way to Buck Island a big rain squall seemed headed directly for us but Bomba skillfully maneuvered the *North Star* around it and only a few drops caught us. Out in the sun again with the old boat pushing on its course, Bomba touched my arm.

"Pull-eze suh take de hel-um."

He went below and passed up cans of beer he had in a big compartment full of ice. We had paid $5.00 a head for the excursion and this included all the beer anyone wanted. (See Chapter XVII)

Government-owned Buck Island is a mile long east and west and about half a mile across at its widest spread. It rises three hundred and forty feet high and is covered with small trees and scrub. The entire north shore is foul ground with reefs in close and Buck Island Bar lying across the area one and one-half miles from east to west. There is a light on top of Buck Island visible nine miles off.

On the southwest shore is a couple of hundred yards of steep-to swimming beach where a yacht can nose in almost close enough to put its bow on the sand. We anchored in six feet with the bow of *North Star* nearly on shore. It is a warm spot here, with Buck Island making a lee and the sun bouncing off the wide, blindingly white beach. Bomba put the awning up and after a swim we lunched in comfort. This is no place to go without awnings and sun glasses. There is fine snorkeling off all of Buck Island's reefs we were told. We had had so much of this up to now that we thought just sightseeing would hold us for a while.

On the run back to the Comanche pier Bomba snoozed while we sailed the boat. It is always amazing to me how easy a harbor seems once you have sailed in and out of it.

I remember one summer when three boats of us out of Riverside Yacht Club, Connecticut, were sailing briskly down the Sound after a weekend at Nantucket. It was beginning to get dark as we were off Branford, Connecticut, and we spontaneously decided to go in there for the night and stretch our vacations out one more day. We had each read the sailing directions for the harbor but became more and more confused as we drew closer. Of course, not one of us wanted to show any signs of hesitation. We were a husband and wife team to each boat and as the husbands hung on to their respective helms the wives read and reread all about the rocks called Little Mermaid and Big Mermaid, and their relation to the approach. In less time than it takes to write this, boat number one's skipper picked what he thought to be The Mermaids and shot between them with his fingers crossed. Boats two and three followed carrying four very scared people.

Window shopping is a pleasure in Christiansted where Danish arches line the arcaded storefronts. These flagstones were once trod upon by Alexander Hamilton who clerked in this building in his youth.

After we had taken off the sails and turned on our motors to proceed up river we powered toward the Branford Yacht Club feeling rather smug. At the landing we were met by a large crowd of wide-eyed strangers, many of whom were shaking their heads and saying "Well, I'll be damned. Now I've seen everything."

We had sailed over a patch of rocky shoals fifty yards east of where we should have entered. An exceptionally high in-running tide and winds from the south which built things up under us had given us a fathom where there should have been only a foot. We sailed into Branford many times after this both in daylight and pitch darkness and it always seemed easy to find the proper channel (which by the way is just wide enough for one small boat at a time). But memories like our near-miss the first time at Branford tend to make one very cautious of new harbors as time goes on.

K. Helweg Larsen, a Dane who had spent his youth in St. Croix, but hadn't been to the island in forty years, visited it recently and wrote an interesting account of his impressions. In the book, *Caribbean Cocktail,* which he co-authored with Everild Young, he says that there were many moments, walking around Christiansted "when we could imagine ourselves in Copenhagen." Mr. Larsen was a nephew of the last Danish Governor of the islands and should know what he is talking about.

Hazel and I were very much reminded of Copenhagen as we wandered through the streets of Christiansted. Danish archways of stone and stucco overhang the sidewalks everywhere and make a delicious shade as one window-shops the town. I started to count the archways lining nearly every street and gave up as I got into the hundreds.

The old Danish street names still linger. On Kompagni Gade (Company Street), between Dronningens Tver Gade (Queen Crossing) and Kongens Tver Gade (King's Crossing), is the old market place where generations of peasants have brought their produce. A ten-minute walk through the town to the eastward was a boat-yard which we found was not equipped to haul keel yachts. St. Croix yachts had to go all the way to Beef Island to be hauled. We took our walk in the early morning before the town was awake, and passed a large group of laborers climbing into buses at the Public Works Department. These

This is the trimaran *Three Cheers* during spring, 1972 trials off St. Croix prior to a single-handed crossing of the Atlantic. This super-fast yacht was designed and built by Dick Newick.

were all Puerto Rican road workers, the energetic immigrant group who have stepped in to take the best jobs from the congenitally lazy natives. Near the boatyard was a tumbled-down tenement-like building which on closer inspection turned out to be another of the old mansions with the double stairway leading over the carriage entrance. The rows of huge windows now had ramshackle wooden shutters clinging to them from broken hinges. Half the roof was missing on one wing and rusty galvanized iron covered the rest. We were told that the original roofs of Christiansted were shingles imported from the U. S. Hurricanes and fires had long ago accounted for the destruction of the old roofs and now corrugated iron covers every building on the island. This is the sad fact today throughout the eastern Caribbean, with the exception of Martinique where tiles are still imported from France for roofing buildings of all sizes. But even on Martinique the "tin roof" has made great inroads.

The fine old buildings around the wharf area of Christiansted were established as a National Historic Site on March 4, 1952, by order of the U. S. Secretary of the Interior and as such will be preserved as examples of the old Danish way of life.

We watched a couple of sloops unloading produce from St. Thomas. Also at the dock was an ancient 100 foot long schooner, *La Americana* from Ciudad Trujillo, which was unloading cement and would take away cattle. In the deep channel between the quayside and Protestant Cay was a motor vessel preparing to unload prefabricated housing for one of the many real estate developments on the island.

Adjoining the dock area is one of the best preserved forts in the West Indies. This is Fort Christiansvaern which took ten years in the building between the years 1734 and 1744. On a bulletin board near the entrance a notice announced that free-guided tours of the Historic Site originated at the Fort each morning at 10 A.M. So we went in and lingered by the tiny parade ground where a large guest register was opened under a notice asking all visitors to sign. To the right of the signatures column on each page was a space headed *Comments* and we thumbed through the book reading the enthusiastic comments of most travelers who, like ourselves, love all the Caribbean islands.

Most of the comments were similar to the notation of a Mr. and Mrs. John G. Miller of Nashville, Tenn.: "(Second visit) Hope to return each year!" But there were a couple which show just how difficult it is to please everyone. A Mr. G. E. Green of St. Thomas wrote a one-word comment: "DEAD!!!!" A Mr. and Mrs. Theodore C. Rhoades of Great Neck, N.Y. wrote "Turn on the air conditioning." An attorney, C.R. May of York, Pa. wrote "Land Prices!!?!?!"

We thought we had Mr. Green of St. Thomas sized up accurately. He was voicing his pride as one Virgin Islander versus any other. He also probably liked the noise, traffic, night clubs and big hotels of his homeland. We didn't quite follow Mr. and Mrs. Rhoades of Great Neck. We lived at one time in Great Neck and if ever a place needed air conditioning that was it. As for Attorney May, of York, Pa. and his comment, we think he hit the nail on the head and with just the proper number of exclamation points and question marks. We were later to have a real estate tour of the island and see how right he was.

We had a few more minutes before the tour was to start and walked around inside the stockade. Here a large flamboyant was in flower and it practically filled the area with its leaves and blossoms. Under the tree were several pyramided piles of cannon balls and around the quadrangle were several doors with little barred holes near the top of each. I was very much taken aback as I stepped up to peek into one of these and a long black arm reached out as a voice asked "Cigarette please suh?" Fort Christiansvaern's old cell block is still used as a prison for offenders waiting to be tried in the large chamber upstairs used as a courtroom.

At about ten minutes to ten Hazel decided that since no one else had put in an appearance the tour would probably be called off. So she left to do some shopping. Five minutes later a pleasant-looking man in a National Parks Assn. uniform greeted me and we introduced ourselves to each other.

I had heard quite a bit of Herbert Olsen. He knew more about the history of St. Croix than anyone on the island. Mr. Olsen was an American of Danish birth who had long been interested in the Danish background of the Virgins. To equip himself for his present job he had spent two years studying in Denmark, going over old records of the Danish West India Company in Copenhagen and examining old files of the Danish Colonial Office.

We chatted for a few minutes and when it became apparent that there were no other tourists for the tour I sought to excuse myself.

"Let me come back tomorrow or next day," I suggested. "When there may be a group for you to take around."

"Oh no. My minimum is one and unless you would rather go another time I'm prepared to conduct the tour now."

So I had a most enjoyable hour with Mr. Olsen. We both liked to talk island history and were sort of captive audiences for each other.

Columbus discovered St. Croix on his second voyage on November 14, 1493. The greatest of Admirals substituted the native name, Ay-Ay, with the Spanish, Santa Cruz. So impressed had been the Spanish rulers by the success of Columbus' first voyage that they offered him anything he wanted for this one. He had left Cadiz September 25th with a fleet of seventeen vessels and a complement of fifteen hundred men. On the first voyage Columbus had first set foot in the new world on the little island of San Salvador in the Bahamas. On this second voyage he had let the trades carry him six hundred miles farther south to enter the Caribbean Sea between the islands of Guadeloupe and Dominica. Here the fleet anchored in the lee of a small island which Columbus named Marie Galante for his gallant flagship. Next the admiral shepherded his flotilla up the islands until Saba was to windward, at which point he turned west and a day later was off the harbor now known as Christiansted, St. Croix. It must have taken Columbus only a moment to note the tangle of reefs between him and the inner basin here. He was looking for a place to water his ships and by sailing along the shore five miles farther west he anchored the fleet off what looked to be a fresh water river where a large Indian village was located.

SALT RIVER

Today this small river basin is called Saltriver Bay and a reef lies across the entrance. There is a small unmarked pass through the center of the reef. Small craft can, and do come in here. There is a fathom at the pass and two fathoms of good holding mud bottom inside. The place looks like a truly idyllic yacht hideaway on the chart, but we found it very buggy because the inner shores are lined with mangrove swamps.

On the eastern side of the bay is Saltriver Point, a bluff one hundred twenty feet high. Directly four hundred yards offshore is White Horse, a small rock over which the sea is always breaking. There is a channel between the rock and the point where vessels drawing up to ten feet can safely navigate.

The promontory at the western tip of Saltriver Bay is unnamed on today's charts, but Columbus called the little peninsula which juts out here, "Cape of the Arrow."

In Knox's HISTORY OF THE DANISH WEST INDIAN ISLANDS is this amplification:

"It was while Columbus lay at anchor at this island (St. Croix) that he was made fully aware of the fierce and courageous spirit of these natives. During the absence of the boat which had been sent to shore with 25 men to procure water and obtain information a canoe containing four men, two women and a boy coasting from a distant part of the island, came suddenly in full view of the ships. Their amazement at what they beheld prevented them from first seeing the boat which was now returning from shore and making toward them in order to capture the men.

"At first they attempted flight, but this proving impossible, they took up their weapons and fearlessly attacked the Spaniards. The women as well as the men plied their bows with such amazing vigor and rapidity that although the Spaniards were covered with their shields and other defensive armour several of them were wounded. To avoid their galling fire the Spaniards came within grappling range and overturned their canoe; still it was with no little difficulty and danger that some of them were secured, as they continued to defend themselves and use their bows with great dexterity while swimming. One of the Caribs died after being brought on board having been transfixed by a spear. A few days afterward one of the Spaniards died from a wound received from a poisoned arrow which the Caribs had used."

There is no mention in the records as to what the shore party found ashore or whether or not they located the fresh water which runs clear and pure in the small creek two miles up river. It is of interest to note that the first blood to be shed in an encounter between the old world and the fierce Caribs of the new, took place on an island now under the flag of the United States. Right after the skirmish the fleet upped anchors and sailed for La Navidad, Haiti.

The St. Croix Museum Commission has published a chronology of historic dates of which the following is a summary:

1493 Columbus discovers and names the Island, November 14th.

1555 Charles V of Spain directs that the Indians in the Virgin Islands be treated as enemies and exterminated.

1596 Earl of Cumberland on his voyage to capture Puerto Rico passed the Virgin Islands, and describes the Islands as wholly uninhabited.

1600 First English and Dutch colonists come to the West Indies.

1645 Population of the Virgin Islands about 550 of different nationalities, each having its own leader. Same year fight in St. Croix between English and Dutch.

1645 to 1650 English dominating St. Croix

1650 Spaniards with 5 ships and 1,200 men attack at night and murder all men, women and children; take possession of St. Croix. Towards the end of the same year French from St. Kitts in two ships with 160 men took back St. Croix.

1651 Of 300 French colonists two-thirds and three Governors died. Believing their illness due to the jungle, the forests were burned in the dry season.

1664 French West Indian Company organized.

1665 Under the energetic Governor Du Bois 90 plantations were put in cultivation with such crops as tobacco, cotton, sugar cane and indigo. After Governor Du Bois' death, bad administration, drought and sickness terminated all prosperity and progress.

1695 Population only 147 whites and 623 slaves. Island now abandoned by the French and all colonists were taken to French St. Domingo.

1695 to 1733 St. Croix technically French but uninhabited became a complete wilderness.

Government House in Christiansted is one of the loveliest examples of Danish architecture in the Caribbean. The monogram over the arch of the main door stands for King Frederik VI.

1733 (June 15) St. Croix purchased from the French by the Danish West Indian Co. for $150,000.

1744 (April 16) First Colonial Council consisting of five members met at Fort Christiansted.

1754 St. Croix, St. Thomas and St. John became royal colonies, through the sale of the shares of the Danish West Indian Co. to King Frederik V.

1807-1815 Occupied and held by the British, due to the Napoleonic wars.

1815 St. Croix returned to Denmark in exchange for the Danish island of Helgoland.

1838 The second steam-driven sugar mill put into operation in St. Croix. By 1852 there were 40 steam-driven mills. Before that there were about 70 small wind-driven sugar mills

1848 (July 3) Slavery abolished by proclamation of Governor von Scholten

1864 First negotiation for the purchase by the U. S. of St. Thomas and St. John alone. Earthquake and tidal wave.

1878 Serious riots accompanied by arson and much destruction on the plantations in St. Croix.

1916-1917 Final negotiation for the purchase of the three islands. Agreement ratified both in Denmark and in Washington.

About two city blocks from Fort Christiansvaern is Government House and Mr. Olsen pointed out other buildings of interest as we walked to it. Nearby is the first Lutheran Church of Christiansted, built in 1753; The Danish West India and Guinea Company warehouse, cir. 1746; and the old Danish Post Office built about 1830. It was in the square in front of the fort that Governor-General Peter von Scholten read the proclamation freeing the slaves July 3, 1848.

There is no more beautiful building in the Caribbean than this two hundred year old Danish Government House. Here again the Danish archway motif is prominent. The building forms a U and encloses as fine a tropical garden as may be seen anywhere. There is a pool with water lilies in the center of the garden where many a governor must have paused to meditate.

Mr. Olsen showed me the spacious apartments which once housed the Royal Governors and their families. In the rear wing, second floor was the kitchen with its enormous brick ovens.

In the grand ball room with its mirrors, gilt, and crystal chandeliers one can half close one's eyes and picture the scenes of one hundred fifty years ago when the island aristocracy gathered to toast the birthday of the King. The original furniture of this room was considered so fine that it was transferred to Christianborg Castle in Copenhagen at the time the island became the property of the U. S. The present furniture, mirrors and chandeliers are copies of the originals which the Danish Government recently presented as its gift to the Historic Site Commission. Another recent gift from the Danish Government is a life-size portrait of King Frederick VII which hangs at the end of the room.

When I left Mr. Olsen I visited the St. Croix Museum in the basement of the library. It is small but neatly arranged. The Carib culture which existed on the island when Columbus arrived was completely a stone-age one. All implements from the adzes, with which they fashioned their canoes, to the bowls in which they ground their manioca were made from the native stone. The only signs of artistic endeavor which the Indians left behind was in their pottery. Many of the vessels baked from local clay were decorated with stylized human heads or abstract renderings of fish or birds. There are many good examples of this work in the museum.

A few steps from the museum was Rasmussen's coffee shop where nearly everyone in Christiansted stopped during the day for coffee or a cool drink under the gracious archways. Here I found Hazel and the Dillons having ice cream sodas. I suggested that even though the Dillons were anthropologists off on holiday perhaps they would consent to lead us on a digging expedition. Anthropologists are not necessarily interested in fossil and artifact hunting. This is the bent of archaeologists. But anthropology is the science of man in relation to his origin, distribution, and environment, and the pursuit of this science does not rule out digging. The real trick of digging, especially in the tropics, is to get someone else to do the digging for you while you evaluate what is brought to light.

So I bought Hazel a trowel ("Don't try your gamesmanship on me," she fumed.) and we rented a Volkswagon. The Dillon-Eggleston Salt River Expedition equipped with one trowel and an immense basket of lunch was off.

In Helweg Larsen's book he describes going to the site of the old Carib village at Salt River and in a very few minutes digging up quite a collection of potsherds and arrowheads. This sounded a bit like travel-book romancing to us so we approached our objective with great skepticism. We decided to call it a picnic and if we found a few shells on the beach this would be reward enough for the effort.

We drove the main road west out of town for about four miles and made a sharp right onto the Salt River road leading to the sea. About a mile farther on we met an old man driving a donkey cart and asked him if he knew where Columbus had landed. It turned out he had never heard of Columbus. Visualizing the area as seen from the sea, we drove on to a place where a sugar mill was perched on a low hill above the road and a big padlocked and barbed-wired gate suggested an entrance to the shore. We parked here and with great effort slid ourselves and our gear under the gate. A sign across the road opposite the gate said "Hildermill Estate" but there was no warning to keep out. We walked about five hundred yards through a meadow and along the way passed near some trees where cattle grazed. We noticed that the cattle were not the contented-cow type exemplified by Elsie, the Borden trademark. These looked rather mean.

The shore was piled with coral fragments and the walking east toward the river entrance was not too comfortable. We had originally planned a swim before lunch but reef shallows lined the shore here so that swimming was impossible.

After we had walked about half a mile we came upon a group of women and children sitting in the shallows laughing and splashing. When we asked them to show us where Columbus landed they all unhesitatingly pointed to Salt River Point on the far side of the bay. On a little further questioning it developed that they were visitors from Puerto Rico and had never been in the area before.

At this stage we decided we wouldn't give up until we had gotten to "Cape of the Arrow" so we covered another half mile before we sat down under some sea grape trees to rest. Here the soil had eroded and some shells were protruding from a dirt bank facing the sea.

"Now take your trowel, Honey," I said, "and start collecting potsherds."

Hazel handed me the trowel and as she and Virginia started spreading out the lunch Wilton and I walked over to the eroded bank. I pushed in the trowel to flip an old conch shell out of the clay and with it fell a piece of nicely-molded pottery. In ten minutes we had more pottery fragments than we could carry. In a layer of pottery pieces about three feet below the present ground level a shiny black object was protruding. This turned out to be the cutting edge of a broken stone hatchet. It was beautifully made and is still very sharp after some four hundred years under ground.

After a lunch of cold chicken, stuffed eggs and cucumber sandwiches topped off with some bottles of iced beer, we packed up our potsherds and once again negotiated the sour-pussed cattle and the barbed gate.

Next morning the Dillons dropped by the museum to tell the lady in charge about our expedition.

"You know that Salt River place," Wilton began. But this is as far as he got.

"Oh, no one would be stupid enough to go in there," she said. "There's a herd of Brahman bulls behind that barbed wire. A fellow from New York got in there last week and was chased up a tree. A wonder he wasn't killed before they got him out. Some continentals do the craziest things."

The Dillons let the subject rest there and after exchanging a few pleasantries bought some literature and left.

In recent years St. Croix has become known for its fine cattle. There are presently some eight thousand head on the island and many of these are from fine-strain animals imported from Texas and Wyoming. On Estate Annaly (four thousand two hundred acres owned by Ward M. Canaday of the U. S.) in the lush northwest highlands of the island a breed called Saint Croix Senepol is thriving. This is a cross between the "Red Poll and Brahman," according to a statement issued by Estate Annaly. A few of the bulls were being offered for sale in an advertisement using the following colorful cattle-talk language. "Created in the tropics, for the tropics, through 30 years of cross-breeding. . . . A dual purpose animal which retains the tick-resistant oily hide of the Brahman with the heavy beef conformation of the Red Poll."

Coming and going as we did from the Comanche dock we became acquainted with several of the yachtsmen moored in the basin there. I asked them each a question which had been bothering me. What would they do in case of a hurricane warning?

I knew what we would do. Hurricane-hunting planes have become so efficient with warnings these days that there is usually plenty of time to find shelter. We would do what most of the St. Thomas yachts would do: up anchor and get to Hurricane Hole on St. John as fast as possible. But I was surprised to find that our St. Croix friends said they had good moorings down and would put out plenty of scope and ride it where they were. The Christiansted basin looked to me the last place in the world I would want to ride out a hurricane. And if everyone put out plenty of scope a terrific tangle would certainly follow in such cramped quarters. We had seen so many gales at close hand in recent years in Connecticut that perhaps we were more aware of hurricanes than many Virgin Islanders. We remembered one at Riverside, Connecticut, Yacht Club when almost every mooring failed and boats were flung all over the place. That harbor was snug and well-protected but when the full force of the wind blew in through the tiny entrance and brought with it high water nothing held. There were yachts in the tennis courts, yachts on the rocks, and many that were reduced to kindling. A couple of the lucky ones went inland and came to rest wedged between trees. This happened just at the end of the season and we fortunately had hauled our boat out the week before.

Considering the number of hurricanes which spawn in the West Indies, St. Croix has been singularly favored in attracting few in recent times. St. Croix has suffered only three direct hits in the last sixty years. One smashed across the island on August 7, 1800. There was another October 10, 1916. The last and most recent was on the 12th of September, 1928.

A hurricane visited St. Croix on August 31, 1772, which was of some historical consequence. A local newspaper described this event as

"The most dreadful hurricane known in the memory of man. A few such events would make us all fit for the Kingdom of Heaven. For the Atheist, the Protestant and the Papist would join in unanimous prayer to appease the Lord of Hurricanes."

This catastrophe was so vividly described by a young Christiansted clerk in a letter to his father that attention was attracted to the youth's eloquence and he was sent to Kings College, New York, to complete his education.

"It began at dusk and raged very violently until ten o'clock. Then ensued a sudden and unexpected interval which lasted about an hour. Meanwhile the wind was shifting around to the southwest, from whence it returned with redoubled fury and continued until nearly three in the morning. Good God! What horror and destruction—it is impossible for me to describe—or you to form any idea of it. It seemed as though a total dissolution of nature was taking place. The roaring of the sea and wind—fiery meteors flying about in the air—the prodigious glare of almost perpetual lightning—the crash of falling houses—and the ear-splitting shrieks of the distressed were sufficient to strike astonishment into angels. A great part of the buildings throughout the island are levelled to the ground—almost all the rest very much shattered—several persons killed and numbers utterly ruined—whole families roaming the streets, unknowing where to find shelter—our harbor entirely bare. In a word, misery in its most hideous shape spread over the whole face of the country."

The letter was posted from St. Croix a few days after the disaster, September 6, 1772, and was signed by a man destined for high office in the young republic forming up north, Alexander Hamilton.

The late Folmer Anderson who managed the Bethlehem Sugar Factory on St. Croix for many years, took careful hour by hour notes of the 1928 hurricane as it passed over the island. Here is his note at the height of the storm:

2.00 A.M.   Winds now of hurricane force. Electric cables all down and only lanterns in use. Eastern gallery torn off, part of debris ripping open the roof covering and water begins to drip from the ceilings of all rooms.

Mr. Anderson sums up: "The damage done by the wind was appalling, many coconut palms had their trunks broken 10 to 15 feet above the ground, all buildings were more or less damaged and many mules and oxen killed or drowned in the turbulent streams. No human lives were lost probably because everybody realized the necessity of seeking shelter in the strongest built masonry houses."

Mr. Anderson doesn't mention what happened to the shipping in Christiansted Harbor in this blow and I could find no one around who knew anything about this. Alexander Hamilton had reported "our harbor bare" after the hurricane in 1772 and I imagine it was just as bare in 1928.

The building in which Alexander Hamilton once worked as a counting house clerk is just around the corner from the Club Comanche and now houses the Alexander Hamilton Hardware Company. When we visited the store there was a traveling salesman from Puerto Rico who was trying to revive the old hula-hoop fad by demonstrating his wares to a couple of clerks who were not interested.

"Those things are old hat around here," said one.

The salesman was an intense Latin in a rather zooty suit. As he whirled a hoop around his neck his little Nasser-type mustache twitched violently up and down. Finally wringing wet with perspiration he stopped. "Gentlemen, it's a favor I'm doing you. Thirty million of these things were sold in the States."

"But like the man says, they're old hat around here," said the other clerk.

The Latin picked up his hoops and went away muttering to himself. But he must have found an outlet for a few days later the red, green and yellow plastic gizmos were to be seen all over town.

We went to dinner that night at the Alexander Hamilton Nightclub which is directly over the store. Here in a room just big enough for a bar and a few tables, a ten piece steel band installed itself and went into action just as we were finishing the soup course. As steel bands go, this one was known as the best in the Caribbean. It had won a great many prizes competing with all the other islands. When Admiral Gallery commanded the U.S. Naval base at San Juan he was so impressed with this particular band that he formed the Tenth Naval District Steel Band to compete with it. The din was so overpowering that we paid our bill and left without attempting to finish our meal.

Hula Hoops, nightclubs, loud music—were we losing touch with the magic of the islands? Next day we drove to Fredericksted at the west end of the island and saw some scenery as magical as any in the Virgins.

St. Croix has been called the "Connecticut of the Caribbean." This is partly because so many people from Connecticut have come to St. Croix to spend their winter holidays—and so many who have come to play, have bought land and decided to stay. But also parts of the island look very much like Connecticut.

The drive from Christiansted to Frederiksted is fourteen miles and is easily negotiated in half an hour. We took a couple of hours along the way getting out to look at some of the sugar mills which dot the landscape like the great stone faces of Easter Island. The Centerline Road which bisects the island skirts some low foothills that are very similar to the rolling country around Essex and the Connecticut River —except for the stone mills.

As we drove, Hazel spread a map on her lap—a copy of an old one listing the names of all the original estates.

The word Fancy was a great favorite in naming estates and it simply meant that so-and-so took a fancy to the place. St. Croix has an estate called Fanny's Fancy. Others are Sally's Fancy, Judith's Fancy, Mary's Fancy. Hope was also a favorite. Just outside Christiansted is Anna's Hope. Another estate is Betty's Hope. Others include Eliza's Retreat, Catherine's Rest, Hannah's Rest. One man is memorialized by an estate called Peter's Rest.

Some of the names were romantic: Upper Love, Lower Love, Paradise, Contentment, Solitude, Adventure. Two less romantic were called Jealousy and Humbug. There were several with practical names: Profit, Hardlabor, Work and Rest. Two optimists called their estates Prosperity and All For The Better.

None of the little estates do anything with cane any more. About half way to Frediksted you pass the big present day mill of the Virgin

Island Corporation which sits in the middle of hundreds of acres of cane fields. We were told that 15,000 tons of sugar is processed here in a year of normal rainfall which is around forty-five inches of rain.

Just before we reached Frederiksted we passed close to an old mill and chimney tower which seemed to be in excellent state of preservation. To reach it we drove in a winding dirt road and under some big trees found workmen remodelling a building which was once a very imposing mansion.

An affable colored foreman told us we were on Estate Whim and the old building was being refurbished to become an art gallery and museum. The rooms were enormous and the walls were four feet thick. There was a dry moat around the house which was ten feet across and six feet deep, all built of stone and mortar. The window sills were of white marble. In the cellar we saw the foundations of yellow brick, the same material of which the Danish forts were made and all brought by sailing vessels from Denmark.

We walked through high grass to the mill and chimney and came upon a lot of abandoned and rusting machinery and an old boiler. The mill dated from the very early period when wind turned the rollers that pressed the cane; the chimney dated from the later period when steam power was introduced.

A nice public service could be rendered if one of the tycoons presently developing St. Croix would restore an old sugar mill so we could see how it worked. Compared with modern methods the waste in the old days was prodigious.

In Westergaard's THE DANISH WEST INDIES a colorful picture is painted of one of the early mills in operation at the height of the season.

"The great husky blacks cutting the cane in the fields—Negro boys leading the loaded donkeys to the mill—others carrying in the stalks and tending the crushing, boiling and distilling made a busy scene."

A dozen Negroes were the team necessary to keep a mill operating. Two men fed the cane between the upright cylinders, the rollers of which were made of wood. There was always an axe at hand with which to amputate the arm of a careless feeder whose fingers found their way between the rollers with the cane. Boiling the juice to just the right consistency was a fine art and Negroes who knew how were the most valued help on the plantations. Then as now the residue from the operation was distilled into rum.

As we left Whim we were only a couple of miles from Frederiksted. But just before we entered the town we stopped to stare perplexed at a new house which was being completed and looked as out of place in this setting as a juke box in a Quaker Meeting House. The house did in fact look like a large juke box. It was all spangles and concrete cinquefoils sporting a profusion of colors including much pink and silver paint. A workman told us it was for one of the newly-rich Puerto Rican families. The industrious Puerto Ricans have brought many a good virtue to St. Croix but they certainly do not number among their virtues taste in architecture. A little more prosperity in the ranks of the four thousand Puerto Ricans on the island and the Danish heritage will be smothered in red and silver cinquefoils.

CHAPTER XV

FREDERIKSTED

FREDERIKSTED has the dignity and grace of an old world town on the sea. Here again are all the heavy Danish archways and cloistered walks along the shop fronts. The buildings run about a half mile along the waterfront road called Strand-by-the-Sea. This is no harbor but a completely open roadstead and big vessels have called here for centuries to collect the sugar which is lightered off from the central pier which has a loading crane.

Coming in from the sea old Fort Frederik is prominent immediately north of the landing. The old Danish Customs House is also prominent on the northern edge of town just behind the wharf.

The PILOT states: "The usual anchorage is just off the town on a line with the street passing the Customs House, in five fathoms. The best anchorage is with the fort bearing 099° and Southwest Cape Light bearing 194° in six to seven fathoms. . . . No directions are necessary for making an anchorage off the town, except when rounding Southwest Cape care must be taken not to shoal the water to less than fifteen fathoms. In front of the town the ten fathom curve is less than 0.5 mile offshore. At night keep in the white sector of the light when approaching the town."

There was an eighty foot wooden schooner from Puerto Rico unloading lumber and fruit as we drove out onto the cement pier. Several lighters were moored in a string nearby.

This is not a particularly attractive spot to bring a yacht. But the Frederiksted anchorage would be the place to make for on any dark night when uncertain about finding one's way into Christiansted.

There is nothing "touristy" about Frederiksted. It is a commercial town where inter-island schooners deliver produce and take away cattle, sugar and molasses. Because it is not "touristy" some people like to come to Frederiksted to get away from it all for a few days. A few rooms are available at Victoria House, an old Danish dwelling with a cool tropical patio at 8 Strand-by-the-Sea. This was recommended to us as having especially good food. It was run by Barbara McConnell, daughter of the late Rea Irvin, well-known *New Yorker* artist. We called when Mrs. McConnell was out and it was well past the luncheon period. We had some very good hamburgers and ice cream sodas at the town soda bar next to the Frederiksted Hardware Company.

There is a public bathing beach beyond Fort Frederik, north of town. Beyond this beach there are others as you drive along the shore road. About three miles north of Frederiksted we came to a little cement cabana sitting under some sea grape trees right on the sea beside the road. It had a sign which said *"Sprat Hall,* Recommended by Duncan Hines." The name Sprat Hall sounded like something from THE WIND IN THE WILLOWS. But it was no relation to Toad Hall. The shore front here is called Sprat Hole for the schools of sprat, bait fish, which abound here. We thought a swim would be very much in order and took our suits in behind the cabana to look for the manager. The place was locked up and seemed deserted but soon a small motorboat picked up a mooring off the wooden pier and a bronzed young man rowed in and greeted us.

This was Jim Hurd, the proprietor of Sprat Hall. He was another ex-Connecticut Yankee who came to St. Croix on a visit several years before and stayed on. He married the sister of the one-time governor of the Virgin Islands, John David Merwin. The beach cabana was not Sprat Hall but the shore front of the two hundred acre estate. Mr. Hurd invited us to have a swim and then come up on the hill and see Sprat Hall. The swimming was excellent here in about eight feet of water off the end of the dock. We felt greatly refreshed as we drove to the old mansion on the hill.

We had seen so many ruins of Great Houses on the cruise that we were getting a little tired of the subject. But here at last was a great house intact. Here was a real architectural beauty set in a group of large trees and flower gardens. The house had been in the Merwin family for generations but had been built originally by French colonists in 1670. Later it had been altered under Danish occupation. It was one of the few mansions on the island not damaged in the insurrection of 1878. The arsonists had gathered south of Sprat Hall when they formed the mob that marched on Frederiksted. Mr. Hurd asked us if we had noticed that the first floors of the buildings in the town were of heavy Danish construction while the upper stories were of wood in Victorian style. The arsonists had burned the roofs and wooden second floors off, but the massive ground floors successfully resisted destruction.

In the dining room at Sprat Hall is the entire original set of dining table and chairs from Government House. The Merwins purchased it at the time of the Danish transfer of the islands to the U. S. We thought that Sprat Hall was one of the nicest places we had seen in all the Virgins. The estate is open to paying guests the year round but this was the off season. There had so far been no guests and Mr. Hurd expected none. We admired his philosophy about this. Whereas every other hostelry in the islands runs on two rates—Full rate, December to April; half rate June to November—the Hurds charge full rates year around.

"It isn't fair to penalize the people who come in January and then furnish the exact same service and food for half price to the people who come in October," he said. "And furthermore with our system we get no customers at all for several months and we have time to enjoy ourselves. After all we like the 'relaxed island life,' as advertised in the tourist bulletins, too."

Jim Hurd is an ardent fisherman and told us that Sprat Hall is the only resort in the Virgin Islands catering to fishermen and their families. He claims that there is good fishing of all types available in the waters around St. Croix and he himself caught so many fish last winter that, besides supplying his kitchen with more than the guests could eat, he had enough to sell and give away. Slightly offshore where the water runs dark blue you can get dolphin almost anytime, he says. Inshore, fishing from a boat or the beach with light tackle you never know what will hit your lure: tarpon, pompano, snook, snapper, ladyfish, barracuda and crevalle all abound in the nearby shoal waters.

There is also excellent bottom fishing for grouper, yellow tail, trigger fish, grunts and sea-bass.

Trolling offshore Hurd has caught, besides dolphin, plenty of such game fish as tuna, wahoo, king and Spanish mackerel. Blue marlin are most abundant in the summer months while white marlin and sailfish favor the cooler months.

We have never gone in much for fishing. Few sailing yachts want the mess of bait and gear aboard, let alone the worse mess if something big is caught. But we were fascinated with Hurd's theories which we know very well must work or he would have long since lost the enthusiasm of the dedicated angler.

"There are fishermen who claim that on some days nothing will bite," he said. "But I don't take this premise for granted at all. I've found that one day a fish will take only a yellow feather, the next day only a red and white feather, the next day only a bait-fish. I troll four or five different lures at one time. This is the sure way to find out what they want."

One other thing about the fishing around St. Croix is distinctly different. As has been said before, this island rests on a different submarine shelf than the cluster of Virgins to the North. The warnings on fish poisoning one hears around St. Thomas do not apply here.

I remember the time we had first entered Drake Passage. We were towing a white feather lure. We had towed it for four hundred miles without a strike. It had been the crew's idea and since we caught nothing we figured it was a harmless pastime. Then suddenly, just after we passed Round Rock, something hit the line. I pulled it in and it was a ten pounder which the boys called a "cavally." They said it was generally good eating but taken here it would "scratch." This is the native term for poison and much as their mouths were watering for fish they threw it back. An hour later off Tortola we had a second strike, this time a bonita and they said "okay" and served it for lunch.

There are two schools of thought in St. Thomas regarding fish poisoning. One says to beware of fish caught east of Sail Rock. Another says beware of anything caught west of Sail Rock. Puerto Ricans say that all Virgin Islands fish are apt to be dangerous because they feed on the vegetation, or on small fish who feed on the vegetation, growing on underwater copper banks. At one time there were large copper mines in operation near the Baths of Virgin Gorda so the copper angle is not entirely based on legend.

We had friends in St. Thomas who explained the fish poisoning business as having to do entirely with the length of time elapsed between gaff and galley. They took fish everywhere from Vieques Island, Puerto Rico to Anegada and ate all varieties with no ill effects. But several times when they gave natives some of their surplus the results were disastrous. As they checked up on the hapless peasant who almost died before the ambulance and stomach pumps arrived they found that the fish had been left around a couple of days and allowed to ripen.

In case you are ever doubtful about whether or not the fish you have eaten is "scratching," here are the symptoms: Severe stomach pains and violent retching three hours after the fish has been eaten. Twenty-four hours later you break out in a rash which covers your whole body with red splotches. I have heard of no one dying from fish poisoning but of many who say death would be preferable.

Here are a few of the maximum weights of fish brought in at Sprat Hall in one season. Dolphin—40 lb. Amberjack—70 lb. Wahoo—99 lb. King mackerel—40 lb. Yellowfin tuna—137 lb. When you get tired of fishing in the ocean, Hurd takes you to fresh-water farm ponds where large and small mouth black bass are to be caught all the year around.

One more thing about Sprat Hall that is unique. Nearly all the hotels of St. Thomas and Christiansted are run on what is called The Modified American Plan. In simple language this means no lunches are served; you must go out and buy your lunches elsewhere. When you and your wife are paying $50 to $60 a day for a double room with only breakfast and dinner included, you feel rather taken to have to taxi to some restaurant for lunch at another $6 or so. At Sprat Hall you paid less for a double room and three meals per day.

October is apt to be a hurricane month in the Caribbean but when it is not the weather is as fine as one could wish, with good steady breezes, beautiful sunsets, and calm seas. While we were at St. Croix the body of deep water between us and the main group was for many days as placid as the proverbial mill pond. We watched small inter-island sloops sail north each day and disappear in the gentle swells toward the islands sprawled on the northern horizon. Others came in spanning the sea between St. Thomas and Frederiksted with crews stretched around the decks asleep in the warm sunshine.

At times in the winter months, when the trade is blowing its strongest, it has been known to get very rough in these waters. But these conditions are watched for by small craft and when things are bad they wait a few days for wind and seas to ease off.

There are scores of days each year that we called good hydrofoil weather. We were thinking quite a lot of hydrofoils, for during the summer months we had seen much hydrofoil activity in the Windward Islands.

Our friends, Dr. Frank Calderone and his wife Mary, had been sailing their 60 foot Alden schooner *Tradition* around the Caribbean for several years. On a recent visit to the island of Montserrat the Calderones were impressed that the little community there had thousands of pounds of ripe tomatoes on its hands and the entire crop was spoiling because no transportation was available to get it out. The Calderones went to Italy where a fleet of hydrofoils has operated successfully for years and brought one of the $125,000 craft back with them.

They christened the all-metal ship *Flying Fish* and we had a ride with them in June when they were demonstrating in the waters between Trinidad and Martinique. Watching the islands flash by at 40 M.P.H. in a craft which seems to be like a seaplane about to take off, is a thrilling experience.

The *Flying Fish* was equipped to carry forty passengers and three tons of cargo and it was Dr. Calderone's plan to base a squadron of five of them in a harbor centrally located in the Windwards and eventually expand the fleet and schedules to service the entire Caribbean with fast economical surface transportation.

We were told that there was so much tourist traffic already booked to St. Croix for the season's Christmas Festival that there was a long waiting list for air transit out of St. Thomas. Hydrofoils of the *Flying*

The ruins of this once gracious great house doorway and a few walls were all that remained after the great insurrection of 1878.

Fish class can carry seventy-two passengers each when not carrying freight. With Dr. Calderone's dream in operation a single *Fish* could shuttle the forty miles between St. Thomas and St. Croix on hourly schedules and greatly relieve the bottleneck.

Of course the first question everyone asks Dr. Calderone is "what do you do in heavy weather?" The answer is that the *Fishes* do not go out in really heavy weather, but it is surprising how much they can take skimming as they do over the top of the wavecrests. If overtaken at sea by heavy weather the skipper merely cuts off the thirteen hundred horsepower diesel and kicks on the ninety horse auxiliary diesel which pushes the boat at fifteen knots with the hull running in the water as a conventional boat. Another safety factor, besides the fireproof diesels, is the compartmentation which makes the boat a non-sinkable life raft if all the power should fail.

Latest word from the Calderones was that if they could not get the proper local cooperation to set up a base in the Windwards they were planning to operate out of Puerto Rico. Some time later we heard that the U. S. Coast Guard had granted *Flying Fish* the coveted International Safety Certificate allowing it to operate anywhere within fifty miles of land and the Puerto Rican authorities had made the necessary concessions to ensure the basing of the *Flying Fish* fleet at San Juan.

Guy Reynolds, who managed the Club Comanche, said he was often surprised at the large number of days in the year the sea was very calm between St. Croix and the main islands. It was during conditions such as these that the Indians used to maintain intercourse by canoe between the islands. Guy's friend Ed Dale, who owned the Club Comanche, was in the U. S. while we were visiting so we missed seeing him. Ed Dale knows the waters around St. Croix as few others do, this statement to include even that old pro, Bomba. One of Ed's favorite stunts was to take his 72 foot yawl *Comanche* in and out of Christiansted Harbor at night under sail only.

One dark night the previous winter Guy had noticed a blinker rapping out signals outside the reef. Ed who was a World War II flyer read the message. Two U. S. Navy craft were lying off the harbor looking for a pilot. Dale told Guy to keep flashing from the top of the Club Comanche tower while he Dale, jumped into a canoe and went out over the reef to contact the ships. When he came alongside the blinker he was surprised to see two submarines sitting there. He showed the captains a suitable place to anchor then told them to stand by while he arranged to take the shore party in. Dale then paddled back across the shallows to his yawl, put sail on and went out single-handed to bring the astonished group in.

Dale made sailing around St. Croix seem easy as pie. That it will never be too easy was a thought brought home to us with news of the island a week after we left. Nancy and Bob Scanlon, a couple we had missed at their house on Marina Cay, were making a night passage, sailing their 30 foot cutter *Fancy Free* home to St. Croix from St. Thomas. They overshot St. Croix's west end and came about some miles southwest of Frederiksted. They later picked up the Buck Island light and headed back for Christiansted Harbor. But somehow they got too close, hit a reef and *Fancy Free* went down in minutes. They had just time to get their baby and themselves in their dinghy for the row ashore.

We kept remembering the remark in the guest book at the fort about St. Croix real estate. "Land Prices !!?!?!" So we called at one of the realtor's establishments in town and were given a run-down on current prices.

The lands around Estate Whim, where we had visited the sugar mill at the west end of the island, have been broken up into one-acre plots. Prices here start at $5,000 per plot. None are on the sea and those in the $5,000 bracket are a long walk from the beach, where a community bath-house is located. We were shown a plot on the map which was two hundred feet by two hundred five feet and had been recently bought for $10,000.

One of the most promising subdivisions on St. Croix for people who like the sea is the development at Judith's Fancy. This acreage includes Salt River Point and most of the land bounding the bay on the west opposite the spot we did our digging for Indian relics. It was planned to develop a basin inside the bay here for a small craft anchorage and landing complete with yacht club. Acre plots here start at $4,000, but to get near the sea the tariff jumps sharply upward. We were shown a plot two hundred feet square on a knoll a good iron shot from the sea which had just been sold for $15,000.

Judith's Fancy's original mill and adjacent buildings were extensive picturesque ruins which dominated the middle of the subdivision. A planting program was necessary because so very much of Judith's Fancy was bare rolling land that had lain denuded since the first planters had cleared away everything for cane. Most of the best locations at Judith's Fancy had already been sold to eager buyers from the United States and particularly Connecticut. An ambitious road-building program was contemplated.

When we had finished our real estate inquiries we had a large armful of brochures which collectively told this story: no palm-studded bathing-beach frontage is available on St. Croix at any price short of a king's ransom. The best undeveloped one-acre sites "in view of a beach" might bring anything from $12,000 upwards.

One member of an old St. Croix family who didn't want to be quoted said: "The continentals who have recently subdivided properties on this island truly astound us. They have had the imagination to take plots which we consider absolutely worthless and turn them into million dollar enterprises which other continentals fight to buy at any price. Why, even on the east end of this island where nothing grows the land has gone from a few cents an acre to thousands, just in the last five years."

We drove to East Point, which is the farthest eastern point of land in this hemisphere under the American flag, and stood on the high bluff jutting into the sea. There is a grim lack of beauty here on this arid wasteland where only cactus grows. Yet we were hardly out of earshot of a group of bulldozers rooting up boulders and cactus to stake off a new subdivision at $5,000 per acre. We were told that this newest project was almost completely sold out.

Driving back to Christiansted we stopped at the Buccaneer Hotel which overlooks Beauregard Bay just outside of town. The original building was erected by a Knight of Malta in 1653 and has been recently extensively refurbished. Below the hotel we had a swim at one of the best beaches on the island—one of the few under waving palms exactly as pictured in the brochure.

During our visit we enjoyed a memorable meal in a lovely setting at Hotel-on-the-Cay. They maintain a round-the-clock boat service from the town dock to their private dock. We were ferried over for a swim and had a delicious buffet luncheon on the beach under the trees.

After lunch Alice Yaten, the manager, took us through the house and told us it had originally been the home of the harbor pilots. The cay had first been called Loots Cay which appears to have derived from the Danish word "Lods" which means pilot. The islet came to be called Protestant Cay for the Frenchmen who were given sanctuary on St. Croix at the time of the Huguenot massacres. Around 1778 the pilot quarters were enlarged and the present lovely Danish façade added when the main building was converted into a summer residence for the governors. At least one of the royal governors must have been a fun-loving fellow for there is a flight of stone stairs leading up to the gubernatorial bedroom from outside, so His Excellency (or anyone else) could come and go without passing through the main part of the house.

Mrs. Yaten had an interesting scrap book of island items. One of the clippings was about Bulow Minde, the estate house of Governor Peter von Scholten. This he built for his beautiful mistress, one Anna Haagard, with whom he lived for some twenty years. *Bulow Minde* means "Remember Bulow." The governor was a sentimental man and christened the house in memory of a close friend named Bulow who died in Denmark the year the structure was completed. The von Scholten-Haagard idyl came to an end in 1848 when the slave owners became so infuriated because the governor freed the slaves that they sought his life and drove him off the island. He escaped the island disguised in Anna's clothes and got to Denmark where he died soon after. Anna died of a broken heart a few years later and her ghost is said to be seen roaming the ruins waiting for Peter's return even to this day.

The Hotel-on-the-Cay scrap book also had a typewritten copy of a story called *Captain Martell and His Crew* which was from an ancient tome written by a Captain Charles Johnson and published in London in 1724. The book was sub-headed "A General History of the Most Notorious Pirates" and told how Captain Martell had been taking prizes in Cuban and Jamaican waters and needed provisioning and refitting. So he called at "a small island named Santa Cruz in latitude 18°30′ N, lying southeast of Puerto Rico." His ship carried twenty guns, a captured prize also carried twenty guns and he also had a sloop of eight guns. Aboard the flagship he had £1000 in silver bars taken from a Spanish Caravel he had captured and sunk near the eastern tip of Jamaica.

"Captain Martell warped into a small harbor on the north side of the island. This harbor was cursed by a reef offshore and a small islet lying within the bay. Here they had sixteen feet of water at the deepest and nothing but rocks and sand without, which secured them from the winds and sea and likewise from any considerable force coming against them."

It is recorded that Captain Martell erected a battery of four guns on the brow of the islet where Hotel-on-the-Cay now stands. Another battery was placed on the point across. A picket sloop was anchored at the mouth of the channel to hinder any vessel coming in. With these precautions they went ahead with their refitting.

Meanwhile the British Commander in the Leeward Islands learned of the pirate rendezvous and sent H.M.S. *Scarborough*—thirty guns and one hundred and forty men under Captain Hume to St. Croix to capture Martell and Company. The *Scarborough* arrived off the entrance to Christiansted harbor in the early morning but hesitated in risking the tricky channel. The pirate batteries commenced firing and the man-of-war anchored and returned the fire. The British gun crews must have been off their feed for only after a continuous cannonading until four in the afternoon was the pirate ship in the channel sunk. Martell, at this juncture, decided to try the inshore passage with his flagship and escape but soon ran aground in Beauregard Bay. Here he set fire to his ship and he and his crew disappeared in the woods. " 'Twas probable they might starve, for we never heard what became of them afterwards." But an old map of St. Croix shows that the estate now owned by the Buccaneer Hotel was once the property of a Martell.

Among our pleasant memories of Christiansted are some wonderful meals we had at Mahogany Inn, a block from the anchorage pier. The Inn which accomodated only fifteen guests was owned by an attractive young couple, John and Christie White, who came down on a visit from the U. S. a couple of years before and decided to stay. The beautiful old mansion was a Danish merchant's house erected about 1750. It is built around a cool inner courtyard where all the meals were served under a luxurious growth of tropical trees.

Mr. White was a top-flight architect and had more work on his drawing board than he could possibly handle. But his hobby was cooking and he personally supervised the preparation of everything that came out of Mahogany Inn's kitchen. He told us that once in a while they featured a deer meat stew that was especially flavorful. St. Croix had a breed of deer which had been running wild in the hills since early times. They were small animals about as big as a large wolf hound, and when they got too numerous the authorities allowed hunters to go in and thin out their ranks. Occasionally an over-zealous nimrod would shoot a few St. Croix deer out of season and black-market the meat to the hotels. Only recently the police had information that four hundred pounds of the meat had been sold and they raided a number of deep freezes looking for it.

Mahogany Inn had its treasure story too. Workmen told the Whites that one day when they were transplanting a tree in the courtyard for the former owner they came upon a pit filled with sand covering two iron-bound chests. All workmen were immediately dismissed and no one knows what the owner found. I thought of interviewing the gentleman but was told he now resides in Europe.

Just before we left the island we ran into a most unique brand of hospitality. We were window-shopping along the cloisters in front of The Carib Cellars Liquor Store and Mr. Nelson, the proprietor, came to the door and greeted us.

"I have some strawberry cordial made from the tiny St. Croix berries. Come in and try it," he said.

We were led through the shop to a tasting bar in the rear and spent two hours sampling cordials. The locally-created cordials of strawberry and banana were deliciously smooth. But our tasting-faculties dulled as we joined Mr. Nelson in sipping several other flavors including a black cherry he had recently imported from Europe. He said his cellars contain as large an assortment of liquors and liqueurs as to be found anywhere in the world. He spends several weeks abroad each year scouting the continent for unusual vintage wines. Most Americans think of the duty-free Virgin Islands as a good place to buy scotch and rum only. Mr. Nelson had all the popular brands of scotch, gin and vodka at special prices in case lots, as well as some rare sherrys which he imported from Spain. He had traced a sherry which sold for $29.00 a bottle in the States and found the vintner who made it in Spain. This he sold for $3.95 a fifth. It tasted fine to us but anything would have, after the strenuous routine of sampling we had been put through.

The night before we headed north for St. Thomas the town of Christiansted went wild. A mob pushed through the narrow streets yelling and screaming and an observer in a helicopter might have looked down and thought: "This is it! Thousands of natives are about to fan out over the island and pillage all the rebuilt Great Houses from east to west."

But a closer look would have revealed the smilingest, snycopatingest, shufflingest crowd of celebrants to be seen on city streets since Joe Louis Day in Harlem.

The citizenry of Christiansted were celebrating as they always had, no matter who won, the final of the World Series.

CHAPTER XVI

RETURN TO OUR MOORING

Renegade covered the thirty-six miles from Buck Island, St. Croix, to Buck Island, St. Thomas, in four and a half hours flat, just the time she had taken on the hitch south. With the broad reach each way this is almost too easy sailing.

With St. Thomas' Buck Island abeam we still had about an hour to go before picking up our old moorings at Yacht Haven. As we sat in the cockpit watching the buildings of Charlotte Amalie grow from tiny dots to red-topped cubes we tried to picture what it must have been like when sailing vessels from European ports swarmed in here daily.

European vessels bound for the West Indies used to first steer for the islands off the African coast where the trades embraced them and swept them toward the Caribbean on a journey that sometimes only took four weeks under perfect conditions. Sometimes they took as long as seven or eight weeks to make the crossing. The long crossings were particularly terrible when the cargoes were slaves. On slow crossings the slavers used the food they carried in the limited space provided, sparingly, and their human cargoes would be kept near starvation during the first few weeks then fattened during the final weeks. It was as ghastly a business as man ever perpetrated on man.

Although the Danes bought and traded and used slaves to the hilt, their ships were not engaged in the slave trade. Usual practice was for the Danish sugar fleet to leave Copenhagen in September and October for St. Thomas, and remain there until the winter's sugar cane crop had been harvested. As mentioned before, the ships came out ballasted with Danish brick. They replaced this cargo with casks of sugar with which, they sailed home in April and May heading north to pick up the westerly winds above Bermuda.

Of all the thousands of passages under sail from the Canaries to the Caribbean it has been the lot of the present generation of small-craft yachtsmen to dramatize the fact that it can be done in anything down to practically a wash tub flying a pillow case. The Commodore of the Royal Barbados Yacht Club had told us last year that so many be-whiskered single-handed sailors had put in at Barbados after recent Atlantic crossings that the club members now hardly leave their rocking chairs to greet a new one.

But Eunice had seen a bit of Hannes Lindemann, the single hander to end all single handers, and as we slid toward St. Thomas she outlined what this intrepid young German had done up to the time she had met him in Yacht Haven the previous winter. In 1955 he had sailed a dugout canoe across the ocean from Las Palmas to the Virgin Islands. He might have been satisfied that this feat of endurance and self-torture had never been done before. But no, he set out to kill himself again and in January of 1957 completed another crossing, this time taking seventy-six days at sea in a rubber foldboat. He capsized in storms twice, and lost most of his food and gear overboard; he arrived in St. Thomas a shadow of the man who started out. But now he was the only person who had ever crossed the Atlantic in *both* a dugout canoe and a rubber foldboat. And the only single-hander to capsize twice in mid-Atlantic in a rubber foldboat.

After hearing the Lindemann story of a person who seemed to seek self-torture like a Mexican *penitente,* it is very refreshing to pick up that gay and happy treatise ALONE IN THE CARIBBEAN by Fred A. Fenger.

Eunice had this classic in *Renegade*'s library and we read parts of it aloud. In 1911 Fred Fenger shipped his seventeen foot sailing canoe *Yakaboo* from New York to Trinidad and cruised up to the Virgins. From Grenada to St. Thomas, Fenger says he enjoyed "Five hundred miles of the most delightful deep sea sailing one can imagine. For only thirty of the five hundred miles were my decks clear of water."

Although the *Yakaboo,* with only thirty-nine inches of beam and, weighing less than her skipper (147 lbs.) , had only inches of freeboard, Fenger sailed the rough passages with relish. He made his trip in February when the winds which he parried never blew less than twenty and often "a whole gale of sixty-five m.p.h."

Fenger picked up some weather information from an old Negro which he said may be based on superstition but proved in practice most invaluable knowledge for Caribbean sailing.

The old Negro told him that the secrets of the winds depend on the phases of the moon. Always look for squalls and heavy weather on the 5th day of the moon. Fenger kept careful notes on the weather during his six months in the Caribbean.

"Almost invariably from the third to the sixth day and generally on the fifth day of the first quarter I ran into trouble at sea. It is uncanny the way the moon seems to affect the weather in these parts. Heavy squalls would come on like the beginnings of small hurricanes. Often (at this phase of the moon) I would count four or five squalls at a time whipping up as many spots on the sea to a fury of whitecaps and spindrift."

As far as the navigation is concerned St. Thomas Harbor is one of the easiest ports to enter. After you leave Buck Island you pick up Triangle Rocks with Triangle bell buoy marking four sunken wrecks between it and the shore. The entrance to St. Thomas Harbor lies between Muhlenfels Point on the east and Crowell Point, the southerly tip of Hassel Island on the west. In the center of the entrance is Scorpion Rock, a submerged shoal. The entering range is a straight reach from the sea between Muhlenfels Point and Scorpion Rock—a natural five hundred foot wide channel with a controlling depth of thirty-three feet. There is a plan afoot to remove Scorpion Rock, enlarging the present maneuvering area in the harbor by one hundred and twenty-five acres.

After Scorpion Rock we soon left nun #6 to starboard and headed for Yacht Haven. As we closed with the shore we picked out all the familiar landmarks edging the harbor and beyond.

The three hills, or ridge spurs upon which the town of Charlotte Amalie is built were originally christened by Danish sailors as Mizzen-top, Main-top and Fore-top reading from left to right. Mizzen-top, now called French Hill, is the western spur some one hundred sixty-five feet high. The center hill, Main-top is now called Berg Hill. It is almost three hundred feet high and has a prominent large white water catchment on its western side near its crest. It also has a conspicuous square white building on it. The eastern spur, Fore-top, now called Government Hill, is two hundred five feet high and has a tower on it called Blackbeard's Castle, easily defined from the water. To the eastward of town another "pirate stronghold," Bluebeard's Castle, stands prominently on a hill and surmounts the cluster of white buildings which now house Bluebeard's Castle Hotel.

It is always a shame to prick any legends about pirates, but according to Danish authority K. Helweg-Larsen neither of these "castles" was ever inhabited by pirates. They were watch towers put up to guard the hill approaches behind Fort Christian. The towers, garrisoned with eight Danish soldiers each, were erected shortly after the main fort at the dockside went up in 1671. Since the towers were originally erected to ward off pirates it is probable that in due course they were named for the most prominent of the bearded buccaneers.

We have said that "as far as navigation is concerned St. Thomas Harbor is one of the easiest ports to enter." This was a deliberate qualification for if you happen to be coming in from any port outside the Virgin Islands, St. Thomas authorities may make entry a very difficult proposition.

To begin with you are required to bring your boat alongside the town's main dock near Fort Christian where it is very hot and you are apt to roll a lot of scratches into your topsides. Here health, agriculture, immigration and customs men—a squadron of four—board you. They will not come out to you at anchor as is the practice in other ports of entry. Plenty of pleading letters have gone to Washington about this but to no avail. Recently Commander Nicholson's big schooner *Mollihawk* came in from Antigua and tried to anchor off. She carried an important official of the U. S. State Department and hoped to avoid the pounding in the hot sun at the dockside. But the local authorities were adamant and made her come alongside for the usual long-drawn out rigmarole of questionnaires and queries.

When *Renegade* first came in from the British islands the four horse-men boarded her and the spokesman greeted her with four words: "Where are the forms?"

"What forms?" asked Eunice.

"Forms 43 R and 995 A."

"Will you let me have some to fill out?"

"We don't have any. You are supposed to supply the necessary forms."

"But where do I get them?"

"You go ashore and buy them."

Eunice spent the next four days tramping the streets of Charlotte Amalie trying to locate "the forms." She learned that they are usually stocked by certain grocery stores but the grocers were expecting a change in the forms and so were temporarily out of stock. Form 43 R comes in a pad of forty sheets two feet square and they won't sell you single sheets. The pad is $2.00. Form 995 A is a card and one of each of these was required for her crew. The cards were only five cents but they were as hard to locate as the pads. In desperation she took a taxi out to Yacht Haven and hailed several anchored yachts trying to get the forms. They didn't have any to spare. Bob Crytser, who handled Eunice's charters from Yacht Haven, received a phone call from Immigration saying in effect, "For Pete's sake, can't you do something about *Renegade*? Her entry is not in order."

Bob contacted Eunice and said, "For Pete's sake Eunice, don't be so darned stubborn."

In the meantime *Renegade* lay pounding at the town dock and no one else was allowed to go ashore. Tempers were growing short. Eunice phoned Immigration and tried to explain and was told that she would shortly be subject to a $10,000 fine.

"But I can't get the necessary forms," she pleaded.

"That's your problem," came the answer. At length she went to Cryt-ser's office and the two of them carefully searched every filing cabinet he had and came up with one of the large forms and six cards. The crisis was past.

This was all just the reverse of going into British entry at Tortola. There on any piece of paper at hand—any size—any color—you merely write *"Renegade,* American sailing ketch, 19 tons" and list the names of the people aboard. This is handed to the lone official who comes out to your anchorage, and nothing else is required.

But we hadn't gone outside the Virgins this trip so our entry was fairly uneventful. A big cruise ship was tied up at West India Dock and started landing its six hundred passengers. Soon a long line of tourist laden taxies was headed for the famous shops of St. Thomas.

Speaking of cruise ships, during recent years passenger ships flying the flags of all sea-going countries, large and small, have gone into the business of carrying tourists into the Caribbean during the winter season. Some of these call at the islands in the sun all year round. But the busiest months for cruise ships are December through March.

St. Thomas had long been a favorite port of call for the Scandinavian holiday ships which were built for the purpose. But in recent years, as jet planes stole the passenger revenues from ocean-crossing shipping, the giant liners turned themselves into floating hotels bound for the tropic isles. Even such a relatively less-known island as St. Lucia suddenly found its cruise ship visits had increased in number from five calls a year to one hundred thirty. Seeing the *Elizabeth II* and the *Rotterdam* both lying off the tiny Castries Harbor at the same time was an awesome sight, especially for the St. Lucia fishermen sailing out of the harbor in their dug-out canoes.

There has always been quite a bit of rivalry between the tourist boards of the various Caribbean islands. Board members closely follow the trend throughout the season and when you hear a group of them talking it sounds like the scoring of some kind of a game.

"I hear Barbados got four last week," says one.

"Martinique got five," says another.

"St. Thomas got six," says a third.

"But those four at Barbados were not big ones."

"No matter. They had the *Europa* and the *France*, and the Royal Yacht *Britannia* the week before last."

CHAPTER XVII

ST. THOMAS, TORTOLA,
and others, REVISITED

One morning during a 1972 visit to St. Thomas we decided to walk the entire inner shore line of Charlotte Amalie harbor from our hotel at the western end, to Yacht Haven at the eastern end. It was a leisurely walk which took us about an hour as we rubbernecked along the way—we wanted to see how much things had changed since we had first visited the island. Some things hadn't changed a bit. Along the city's dockside were the usual old beat-up sloops from the outer islands vending their wares to curious locals. One sloop had a deck load of green coconuts which were hacked open to be sold to thirsty pedestrians. Another offered a display of polished shells of young turtles. A small motor launch was loaded with a catch of bonita weighing three and four pounds apiece. The skipper and mate of this craft were very busy weighing and selling the fish, as fast as they could keep up with the queue, at 50 cents per pound.

But aside from these glimpses of the past plenty of changes had taken place. On the shore front next to Cha Cha Town was a new marina featuring yacht charters, hauling and repairs. This operation called Avery's Boathouse, Inc. stated in its advertising "We have the Caribbean's finest Bareboat Fleet at our dock." Average weekly rate for this do-it-yourself cruising was $600. for a party of six in a 35 ft. Pearson sloop.

Walking along from Avery's we passed the busy air-boat ramps servicing the fleet of flying boats that connect St. Thomas with San Juan and St.

Croix pretty much around the clock. The roar of the sea planes taking off and pulling up on the ramps made the air around Cha Cha Town a bedlam of noise. This operation, Antilles Air Boats, advertised itself as the "World's largest Seaplane Airline." Next along shore was the ferry of Tortola, the *Bomba Charger*. Adjoining the ferry waiting-room was a ticket office bearing a large sign announcing hydrofoil services between St. Thomas and the British Virgins. The ferry boat ticket man told us that the hydrofoils (7 of them) had operated only for a few months. The firm had gone bankrupt and someone had forgotten to take the sign down. A typical West Indian situation.

Across the shoreside boulevard from the ferry we dropped in at the huge modern Windward Passage Hotel. This was during the last week in April—carnival time—and every room was filled. The hotel had a large inner court lined with shops. We were amused to see the steady stream of gaily bedecked tourists carrying six-pack cartons of bargain vodka, rum, gin and whiskey from "Mr. Woodie's" block long bazaar to waiting taxies. As we walked nearer to the center of the harbor a large cruiser full of tourists from the Rockefeller hotel on St. John came alongside for a landing. This was on a Monday, the specified day for the guests at Caneel Bay to visit Charlotte Amalie and shop for liquor and straw hats. Near the cruiser's landing place was the glass-bottom boat operation. These two craft were made up to look like minature stern-wheel river boats, and were gaily painted. Fish-watching had always proved to be popular as a tourist attraction and the boats were busy plying to and from the coral gardens.

The sun shone brightly but we were refreshed by the trade wind as we walked another half hour to Yacht Haven near the old West Indian docks. There two cruise ships were unloading their hundreds of tourists to waiting taxies. But the famed Yacht Haven Hotel was undergoing some monstrous changes to be completed by the mid 1970's. A high wire fence surrounded the building complex, and the original swimming pool and yacht club area. Demolition squads were busily at work knocking everything down. The original marina was, as usual, crowded with yachts of all types for charter and sale. An official of the marina told us that some 300 yachts were in the area. A folder made the claim that Yacht Haven Marina sheltered the "largest charter yacht fleet in the Caribbean." We were also told that new plans for the area envisioned new docks, new piers and a shopping mall with a series of

[195]

high rise condominiums ringing the shoreside. Several yacht skippers told us they looked forward to the changes with horror.

When we think of yachts and yachting in tropical waters we usually do so with envy for those who are able to live this life—so footloose and fancy free. This was true of *Renegade* and many other yachts in the Caribbean that kept moving because their owners loved to sail whether they had a party of friends or a charter party aboard; and even if they chose to cruise alone.

For scores of other yachts, however, the owners and their families live in a marina community as though it were a large auto-trailer camp. Children, dogs, cats and parrots are raised, lettuce is nursed along in boxes on the decks. The early morning at dockside is like a small town coming to life. Dogs bark, young babies cry, older children come popping out of various hatches like so many prairie dogs. Skippers come on deck and send children off to the showers with soap and towels and tooth brushes. Children returning from the washrooms are told to dress for school. Through it all the aroma of bacon frying and toast toasting rises in the morning air to drift over the fleet as busy boat-wives pass steaming plates up the companionways into the awning-covered cockpits. After the line of book-laden youngsters marches off the dock to get the school bus, things steady down to a more quiet routine. Skippers try to keep ahead of the ever-demanding work on their boats. One will have part of a generator on deck trying to make a repair. Several will be sanding and varnishing. Two will be in their dinghies with long brooms trying to scrape some of the "sea grapes" off their hulls. One will be up his mast trying to rewire a spreader light. Some will appear to be sitting and thinking. Others will be just sitting.

About 10 A.M. several of the wives will appear with shopping baskets to visit the nearby supermarket, or join a taxi pool for town. The wives are young and pretty and one wonders how they have managed such fresh-looking clothes in the cramped quarters below. In the height of the charter season, January through March, many of the wives and children live ashore while their husbands sail tourists around the islands. Many of the yachts do not charter; the owners live on them as houseboats the year around.

At Yacht Haven every type of boat from racing sloop to houseboat could be found for charter—and at prices ranging from $300. to $1,000. per week. Prices obviously vary depending on whether the charterer skippers the boat himself or takes along the captain and any necessary crew.

ST. THOMAS, TORTOLA, and others, REVISITED

The Virgin Islands charter people make a good case for their assertion that the total cost per day for a charter party of four compares favorably with the total cost per day for a party of four staying in one of the better hotels.

WATER ISLE. We were fascinated by the changes that had taken place on Water Isle. Mr. and Mrs. Walter H. Phillips, the original leasees had continued to live on and love the isle. Our old friends Tom and Marnie Ford also bought a retirement home there, with a breath-taking view to the southwest. They had left St. John because it was getting "too crowded."

When Walter Phillips first set foot on Water Isle in 1951 he wrote "not one person lived there, and the sole inhabitants were goats, iguanas and termites." The islet had long been owned by the West India Co. Ltd. and never developed. In 1944 the U.S. Government had purchased the property for $10,000. and started to build a fort on it. Work stopped at the war's end and both the Federal government and the V.I. government looked for someone to take it over and develop it. The Phillipses subsequently signed a 20 year lease submitted by the Department of the Interior. The lease stipulated that the leasees develop Water Isle as a resort area comprising a 50 room hotel and private homes, and invest a minimum $200,000. in the first 5 years.

When Mr. Phillips drove us around the isle in the Spring of 1972 we were amazed at the changes that had taken place since the date of our first visit in 1958. Some sixty homes had been constructed during this period. And over 150 subleases had been made to people who intended to build retirement homes. As the Phillipses passed retirement age they decided to turn the further expansion of the hotel operation over to someone else. With the consent of the Department of the Interior a new company was assigned the lease on the hotel area. This multimillion dollar complex now comprises several many-arched main buildings with 120 air conditoned rooms overlooking 20 handsome housekeeping villas.

The householders outside the periphery of the hotel have the utmost privacy. And thanks to the influx of money the once small rocky beach area has been transformed into one of the finest bathing strips in the islands. Also thanks to the efforts of Mr. and Mrs. Phillips hundreds of coconut, fruit and flowering trees were planted on the Isle to replace the ravages caused by hundreds of years of goats. Mr. Phillips' special interest is in orchids, and the

Water Isle Botanical garden has long been a famous focal point for tourist from everywhere.

A trip from St. Thomas to Tortola on the *Bomba Charger* was an experience we were advised not to miss. Over the years many a decrepid ferry had covered the route between the U.S. and British Virgins. The *Bomba Charger*, a vessel expecially designed for the job was powered to cruise at 25 MPH. It was in immaculate condition (a rare virtue in any public conveyance in the West Indies), had a carrying capacity of 90 persons and was 65 feet over-all.

As we sped along the south shore of St. Thomas one after another of the formerly deserted beaches and headlands were now abustle with new hotels in operation or bulldozers readying the land for new foundations. Looking inshore as we passed between the eastern tip of St. Thomas and Great St. James Islet there seemed to be houses dotting the hillsides and shore front in every direction. Cowpet Bay sheltered a small forest of yacht masts near the St. Thomas Yacht Club pier. Then as we approached closer to St. John we were again surprised to see all the buildings on the uplands adjoining Cruz Bay. Cruz Bay had seen few changes since we had first anchored in it. Sewers department store continued as a fixture of the village. A few supplies were still available to yachtsmen, notably ice and some canned goods. Near the local ferry landing was a National Parks service information office and a rental agency for drive-yourself jeeps. Whatever happened to the "Peoples Development Corporation of St. John" was not known.

After one leaves Cruz Bay and Caneel Bay Hotel to starboard and steers for The Narrows between Great Thatch and St. John's Mary's Point, one sees the virgin mass of St. John as preserved through the far-sightedness of one man, Mr. Laurance Rockefeller. When at some future date every island in the Caribbean is scarred with high-rise condomimiums and every beach is dotted with hotels, here will be one treasure of nature left for man to gaze upon—just as God created it. No matter what the "People's Development Co." does with the small area around Cruz Bay, the thousands of untouched acres, and miles of lovely beaches which Mr. Rockefeller turned over to the U.S. as a National Park will stand as a memorial to his generosity and good judgement.

The ferry took us past Little Thatch which we were told had changed hands a couple of times and was still functioning as a hotel. On the shore of

Great Thatch was a grim reminder that care should still be taken in these well-marked waters. The bow and part of the cabin were the only visible remains of a power cruiser which had ripped out its bottom on a rock.

As we closed with the goverment dock at West End, Tortola, we noted another sad sight. One of the out-of-commission hydrofoils lay forlornly at the dockside with just a scrap of the torn red bunting of a Red Ensign dangling from her stern mast. Paint was peeling off the bow of the once sleek 60 passenger craft, but her name *Raketa* could still be read. And on her cabin trunk was the lettering *B. V. I. Hydrolines.*

TORTOLA. Taxies were on hand at West End. They took us to Road Town over the fine water-level strip of highway which was completed in 1966 for the visit of Elizabeth II and Prince Philip. Their visit was commemorated with a plaque at the dockside where the Queen stepped ashore from the *Britannia.*

Road Town has had many shots in the arm in recent years including the addition of several banks and new restaurants. We visited Fort Burt and talked to Paulina Stewart who purchased the property from the Hammersleys in 1967. Mrs. Stewart had most of the original structure taken down and replaced everything with a decor of teak and field stone which together with her planting turned the place into a gem. The accommodations were purposely limited to take only twelve people. Mrs. Stewart explained to us that although it was not economically sound to keep the place small she was happier with it that way.

Under the wide veranda at Fort Burt is the present enlarged Tortola Yacht Services dock, marine railroad, and mooring facilities. Farther north along the shore is a condominium and marina complex called The Moorings. A bare boat fleet is maintained at this marina as well as waterfront apartments. Here are the usual amenities for yachtsmen: ice, hot showers, laundrymat. From this marina a power boat can be hired complete with diving equipment to visit the wreck of the British ship *Rhone* off Salt Island.

From Road Town we taxied out to see the C. S. Y. (for Caribbean Sailing Yachts) marina at Maya Cove. Here we saw functioning one of the busiest bare-boat operations in the Caribbean. At Maya Cove some 38 yachts were on hand to be stocked with every conceivable luxury from champagne to new stereo tapes, for the sailing couples who like to sail the boat they charter without the help of a skipper or crew. We had been flattered that John Van

THE VIRGIN ISLANDS

Ost of Tenafly, New Jersey, who pioneered the large-scale bare-boat business, said he first became attracted to the Virgin Islands by reading a first edition of this book. How Mr. Van Ost could operate complicated marinas on Tortola and St. Vincent and the Bahamas—all whilst he conducted a successful practice as a dentist in New Jersy was for us one of the mysteries of all time. We have found that owning one yacht at a time-no matter how new and perfect—always presented a routine number of headaches. How could John Van Ost possibly handle a million dollar fleet at such long distance? His manager at Maya Cove provided us with some of the answers. John Van Ost of course always made several trips to his marinas each year. His managers did the rest. Andy Douma was in charge at Maya Cove at the time of our visit. Douma explained things in very simple terms. The boats were standardized with interchangeable equipment. The warehouses at the Marina were constantly restocked with wholesale orders of supplies.

While we were visiting, C. S. Y. boats were constantly coming and going. We saw more sails on the horizon than we had ever seen before in this area. We inquired about boat damage and Douma explained that in the two years he had been with the company only three boats had gone on the rocks. Two required minor repairs. One that ran on Johnston Reef required major hull patching. But in that two years some 12,000 people had used the boats—quite a record. A fully stocked Capri 30, a Sparkman Stephens design with accommodations for two couples, was $700.00 per week.

PETER ISLAND. This lonely hide-away islet saw some dramatic changes after Sir Brundel Bruce and his family moved away. The Norwegian-based company, mentioned earlier, built a forty-unit hotel and marina on Sprat Bay. The development was christened Peter Island Yacht Club and was rather quaintly described in a brochure as "An Intimate cottage-colony hotel reflecting the simplicity of the West Indian atmosphere and the amenities of a truly first class hotel without leaving unnoticed, by means of architucture or operation, that its proprietors descend from Scandinavia."

The Scandinavian influence is immediately apparent in the architecture, the decor, and the furnishings. Three shiploads of prefabricated elements went directly by sea from the port of Stavanger, Norway, to Peter Island. Thanks to an arrangement made with the British Virgin Islands Government a team of twenty skilled Norwegian craftsmen was allowed to live on Peter Island and work with the local labor until the job was completed. Two Norwegian chefs were later imported.

Of special interest to yachtsmen was the erection of a slipway to take boats up to twenty tons. Also for yachtsmen, very fine docking facilities were built, with a well protected mooring area.

The Club-Hotel established a daily launch service to Tortola. U. S. tourists visiting Peter Island can be flown from St. Thomas to the landing strip at Beef Island where they are met by a car which takes them to the launch-dock. The launches do the four miles between Tortola and Peter Island in twenty minutes.

VIRGIN GORDA. The western shore of this island, that had for so long been shunned by yachtsmen seeking an overnight anchorage, experienced a change at the hands of Laurance Rockefeller when he constructed Virgin Gorda Yacht Harbour near Spanish Town. Billed as the largest marina in the British Virgins the management announced the creation of dockage space for 150 yachts—plus a restaurant, a bar, ice, showers and all the usual services. Virgin Gorda Yacht Harbour is under the direction of the management of the other Rockefeller operation on the island, Little Dix Hotel. Like the Caneel Bay complex the sixty-six room hotel is very beautifully done. Also as at Caneel, jackets and ties are worn at dinner. The hotel is named for nearby Little Dix Bay but this bight is not recommended for visiting yachts. Yacht parties calling at V. G. Yacht Harbour can taxi the short distance to Little Dix. Tourists visiting from the mainland can be flown from St. Thomas and landed at the air strip near Little Dix.

ANEGADA. According to legend Anegada had not a soul living on it until late in the seventeenth century. This was about the time that the Spanish galleons bound for Panama changed their sailing pattern. They had for a century followed the practise of entering the caribbean Sea around Guadeloupe and Dominica. About 1700 they changed their route of approach to enter the Caribbean between Anguilla and the Virgin Islands. Thus as this new route brought them fairly close to Anegada, ships were soon strewing their bones on the surrounding reefs. This brought the first settlers to Anegada island. These few "first families" salvaged the wrecks and fished and gardened a bit in between. Up to the present time some three hundred vessels have come to grief at Anegada—including S. A. (Huey) Long's first yacht *Ondine*. Although it had long been known that a strong northwest current was the culprit responsible for making so many capable navigators look foolish, the wrecks continued to multiply.

Robert F. Marx, an authority on marine archaeology, spent several years studying admiralty records in England and Spain and noted that of forty-five ships known to have been lost at Anegada prior to 1824 several were British men-of-war. In the writings of Pere Labat (1722) the good padré tells of a Spanish galleon laden with treasure which was wrecked at Anegada. The bulk of the treasure was supposed to have been buried on the island and diggers over the centuries have looked for it in vain.

In recent times scuba diving teams from Virgin Gorda have searched the reefs of Anegada and come up with a variety of cannonballs and cutlasses from several wrecks discovered on Horseshoe Reef. But so far—no gold.

Treasure will supposedly be extracted from Anegada in another way— tourism. A tiny air strip was enlarged, a twenty room hotel erected, and a new jetty constructed at Setting Point.

ST. CROIX. On our refresher trip to St. Croix we checked in at the Club Comanche on the water front as before—and found the hotel expanded and full, with Ed Dale still in charge. Ed had long since replaced his original *Comanche*, the 72 foot yawl, with a larger *Comanche*, a schooner. The first person we called was Dick Newick who with his wife Pat had left the Beef Island yacht yard and settled in St. Croix to become a leading national figure in the design and building of trimarans. Dick started driving us around the island with a call at the waterfront to shake hands with Bomba who continued to sail his *North Star* (thoroughly rebuilt by Newick's yard) to Buck Island. But in the decade of the 70's Bomba will no longer be a lone skipper on the run. Buck Island Reef is now a National Monument and everything that floats plys between Christiansted and the islet daily. More than 50,000 visitors call at Buck Island each year. On many a day the sails on the water in this area look like a Long Island Sound regatta.

Dick had just had a red-letter day. The trimaran *Three Cheers* of his design and build, had departed St. Croix with Tom Follett at the helm to double the Atlantic in a single-handed challenge.

We found that Dick Newick wasn't any happier than any of the old island hands about the influx of condominiums and high-rise buildings come to bless the island. The quaint Hotel-on-the-Cay that had once so charmed us with its ferry rowboat with-the-fringe-on-top, had grown to a massive complex with power boat taxi service and rates for a double room in season beginning at $60.00 per day with breakfast only.

Dick drove us up to see the lovely house he had designed and built overlooking Christiansted Harbor. After a visit with Pat and their two teenage daughters we drove out to the Grapetree Bay area which had looked like such a rocky barren landscape but a few years before. Over the years the owners have managed to make this development look as lush as the early brochures promised with their visionary paintings. The Grapetree Bay Hotel and adjoining Beach Hotel were the fulfillment of a dream by Mr. Fairleigh S. Dickenson of New Jersey. A short drive from Grapetree Bay and back to the north shore facing Buck Island is the handsome St. Croix Yacht Club. There is no finer example of Island Yacht Club House and facilities anywhere in the world. With an assist from Mr. Dickenson the club acquired a perfect beach. The grounds, housing and marina represent some $250,000. Membership is 300. On the moorings and at the piers are some 100 boats of all sizes.

On a visit to Frederiksted we were pleased to find Sprat Hall, the island's oldest great house, still running under the same management and still at reasonable rates. Enroute along the highway west we passed Whim Great House which had been very much refurbished and restored making it one of the finest museums of its size to be seen in the Caribbean.

Back in Christiansted we were sad to note that the "Alexander Hamilton Hardware Store—founded 1750" had been completely gutted by a fire which had fortunately been confined to its walls. Rasmussen's hangout had changed its name to Dolphin. We had a final lunch in the cool patio of Mahogany Inn. The food was superb—as it had been the first year it opened. Anyone who knows the West Indies will tell you that this was the rarest of experiences.

A continuing project throughout the town was the chipping off of the old mortar that had originally covered all the Danish archways. This revealed the beauty of the pale yellow Danish brick that had come out as ballast in the 18th century.

Besides the lovely old architecture to be found on St. Thomas and St. Croix, and the scenery to be encountered throughout the archipelago, there is a special something about the U. S. and British Virgin Islands. A well-known yachtsman who knew well the waters of the South Seas, the Mediterranean and the Caribbean stated it thus: "There is no tropical island blue-water sailing to be found anywhere in the world to match this area with its steady breezes and hundreds of beach-lined anchorages."

INDEX

INDEX

INDEX

INDEX

INDEX

INDEX

10/4

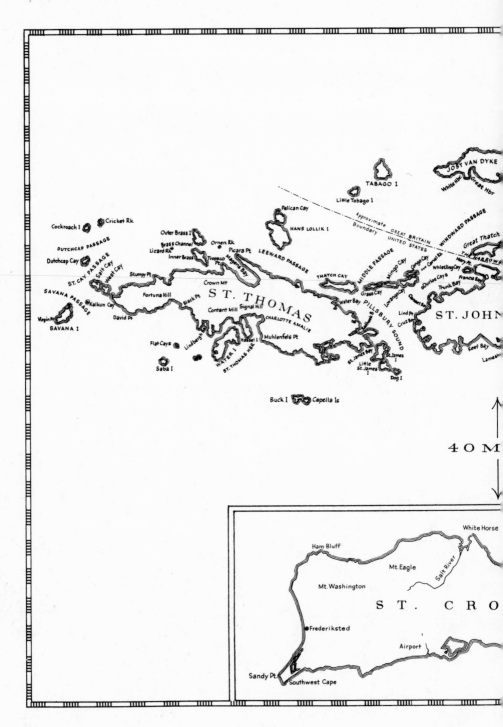

JOST VAN DYKE

TABAGO I

Little Tobago I

White Hrs. Great Hbr

Pelican Cay

HANS LOLLIK I

Approximate GREAT BRITAIN
Boundary UNITED STATES

WINDWARD PASSAGE

Great Thatch

Cockroach I   Cricket Rk

DUTCHCAP PASSAGE

Outer Brass I

Brass Channel

Lizard Rk

Inner Brass

Ornen Rk

Picara Pt.

Tropaco

Magens Bay

LEEWARD PASSAGE

THATCH CAY

MIDDLE PASSAGE

Mingo Cay

Congo Cay

oGrass Rk

Whistling Cay

Mary Pt.

NARROWS

Dutchcap Cay

ST. CAY PASSAGE

Salt Cay

West Cay

Stumpy Pt.

Crown Mt

ST. THOMAS

Water Bay

PILLSBURY SOUND

Grass Cay

Lovangong

oDurloe Cays

Trunk Bay

Francis Bay

SAVANA PASSAGE

Kalkun Cay

Fortuna Hill

Black Pt.

Contant Mill

Signal Hill

Cinnamon Bay

Cruz Bay

Lind Pt.

ST. JOHN

Virgin Pt.

David Pt.

SAVANA I

Flat Cays

Lindberg

Hassel I

Muhlenfels Pt.

St. James Bay

St. James I

Reef Bay

Saba I

WATER I

ST. THOMAS HBR.

Little
St. James I

Dog I

Lameshur

Buck I   Capella Is

40 M

White Horse

Ham Bluff

Mt. Eagle

Salt River

Mt. Washington

ST. CRO

Frederiksted

Airport

Sandy Pt.

Southwest Cape